Lessons
Learned,
Hopefully

Essays about life experiences and the
lessons derived from those experiences

JOHN MCMULLEN

Copyright © 2016 John McMullen.

All rights reserved. No part of this book may be reproduced, stored, or transmitted by any means—whether auditory, graphic, mechanical, or electronic—without written permission of both publisher and author, except in the case of brief excerpts used in critical articles and reviews. Unauthorized reproduction of any part of this work is illegal and is punishable by law.

Scripture taken from the Holy Bible, NEW INTERNATIONAL VERSION®. Copyright © 1973, 1978, 1984 by Biblica, Inc. All rights reserved worldwide. Used by permission. NEW INTERNATIONAL VERSION® and NIV® are registered trademarks of Biblica, Inc. Use of either trademark for the offering of goods or services requires the prior written consent of Biblica US, Inc.

ISBN: 978-1-4834-4820-6 (sc)
ISBN: 978-1-4834-4821-3 (e)

Because of the dynamic nature of the Internet, any web addresses or links contained in this book may have changed since publication and may no longer be valid. The views expressed in this work are solely those of the author and do not necessarily reflect the views of the publisher, and the publisher hereby disclaims any responsibility for them.

Any people depicted in stock imagery provided by Thinkstock are models, and such images are being used for illustrative purposes only. Certain stock imagery © Thinkstock.

Lulu Publishing Services rev. date: 3/18/2016

Table of Contents

Dedication vii

Foreword ix

The Legend Of Joe Thorp 1

Job Descriptions 3

Saying "No" To A Good Idea 6

Leadership Vs. Management 10

Life Isn't A Bumper Sticker 12

Golf Lessons (A Parable About Change) 14

The Cost Of Doing Business 17

Fishing With Uncle Joe 21

We Are Doing This So That… 23

Everything Will Be Fine If We wake Up Tomorrow And It's 1955 25

A Needed Loss Of Certainty 27

Prayer On An "As Needed" Basis 29

Neighbor? Which Neighbor? Who is My Neighbor? 31

Altar Calls 34

Good Words Lost 37

The Importance Of Vision 39

A Better Christian Than You 41

Ministry As A Shared Reality 44

The "It's All Right" People 46

Survival Is Not Mandatory 48

A Marathon, Not A Sprint 50

If I Had It To Do Over Again, I Would Take A Day Off 52

Farther Along 54

Welcome To The NFL 57

But Who Gets The Credit 59

The Value Of Story 61
It's Okay Not To Believe All The Time 63
God Is More Than You Know 65
Don't Let Me Resign In October 67
Happy And Unhappy 69
From Darkness To Light 71
It's Odd What We Remember; It's Odd What We Forget 73
Some Christmases Are Just Harder Than Others 75
Lives That Matter 77
I Would Know Him Anywhere 79
Specific, But Not Necessarily Correct 81
Love, Lost 83
From The Bleachers 85
Whose Side Are You On? 88
What Were You Thinking, God? 90

Dedication

To my wife, Fara
To my children, Stephanie and Michael
To my grandchildren:
Noah, Mackenzie, Sam, Annie, Macon, and Scarlett
To my mentors in the faith and all the people in the
churches I have served who taught me so much.

Foreword

I have decided on several different occasions since I retired to try my hand at writing down some thoughts and memories. It took until now to actually put words on paper. On most mornings I read a bit and then sit down and write. I try to do that first, else the rest of life will interfere as it has so many times before. My intention is to continue the practice for a while.

The question arises as to what to do with what I have written. I initially intended to print it out and share it with the individuals who participate in our Conference's Local Pastors' School each year. I have been one of many who offer sessions during that two-week academy, and basically I have been offering the same course for years which includes observations and lessons learned through reading and experience. Several times on the long drive back from Cathedral Oaks outside of Weimer, Texas, I have thought that the ideas from all those conversations and all those questions answered and discussed might be good to share. So my initial hope was to share what I write with that group of new clergy to serve as a reminder of our conversations together.

But, I also have been impressed by some things others have shared. Some old friends have suggested that I should write down some of my thoughts and memories and share them. Now I have begun to do that in the hope that some of this might be helpful to someone else and that any ensuing discussion can enrich what I have to share with others. There is no particular order to this collection. (People who know me will not be surprised by this.) They appear pretty much in the order in which they were written.

Having been a preacher for over forty years, I feel a need for titles, and I have come up with one for all this: "Lessons Learned, Hopefully." It offers what is the truth for me on several levels. There are so many things that hopefully I have learned, and I am always hopeful that there is more to be learned.

So however you see this and any that might follow, I hope you find it helpful. Everything I know has been shared with me by others through their writing, or through our interaction. It seems the least I can do is to share it with others.

The Legend Of Joe Thorp

I never thanked Joe Thorp, and I should have. I should have thanked him for what he taught me.

It was August of 1972, and we were several days into unpacking and moving our belongings into the parsonage of the United Methodist Church of Mertzon, Texas, a booming metropolis of some 550 people and many more cattle and goats. I was newly appointed to the church there in the county seat of Irion county as well as the church in Christoval some thirty-five miles away. In the midst of our getting settled, the word came. I can't exactly remember now how or from whom. "You need to go see Joe Thorp because Joe Thorp is going to die."

Here it was, my first pastoral call as the head pastor of my own congregation. Oh, I had made more than a few such calls during the previous two years that I had been an Associate Pastor at Laurel Heights, a large congregation in San Antonio. I had done weddings and buried the dead, all the things that real preachers are supposed to do. But this, this was different. I was THE pastor, the head guy. (I glossed over the fact that I was the only pastor, and that I was also the church secretary, part time janitor as well as maintenance man.)

A sense of self-importance was going through my head as I drove up to the house where I had been told Joe lived. I walked up onto the porch and knocked. After a moment a man came to the screen door, and I asked him if I might see Joe. He answered, "I am Joe." I have to say I was shocked that a man so near death was able to stand upright. Recovering from my surprise, I introduced myself. "I'm John McMullen, the new pastor at the Methodist Church." He paused a moment, looking up and down my 27 year-old frame, and then said with a rather wry look on his wrinkled face, "Oh yeah, you're the kid they sent us that kept us from getting a real preacher."

I learned over time that Joe Thorp was a character, and that he was far from the only one in that wide spot in the road leading from San Angelo to Big Lake. By the way, he was still alive three years later when I moved away.

He might have been kidding the new guy in town, but in retrospect, of course, Joe was right. Oh sure, I had the prerequisite years of schooling, having graduated from two prestigious schools of learning with better than average grades. I had gone through all the necessary interviews, served my probationary time, and done all the other required things which led up to my ordination, and I possessed all the framed certificates ready to hang on the wall of my new, but very small, office to prove it.

I had all that, but Joe was still right. He was "I'm telling you something that you need to remember" right. I was the kid the powers that be sent to the people of Mertzon and Christoval, Texas that kept them from getting a real preacher. I was still wet behind the ears. There was still so much for me to learn and so much more to experience.

There is an African proverb which states, "It takes a village to raise a child." I understand the sentiment behind the adage, but I would personalize it. My version would read, "It takes a community to grow a preacher." And I say that because in the years that followed my encounter with Joe, the two West Texas congregations that I was pastoring, and congregations after them, served as tutors for the development of so many needed skills. They celebrated strengths and tolerated weaknesses. They were sources of ever-greater understanding of not only my calling, but my very humanity. Besides those dear church members, along the way there have always been great friends who were willing to mentor, to listen, to instruct, and to guide my journey. They were my village, they raised me, and I am indebted to them all.

All of which is to say that, even seventy-one years in, I am still learning to be a preacher, a minister, a pastor, although not necessarily the one that Joe wanted. (I am not sure that Joe wanted any preacher at all.) I have come to realize that I need to continue to grow in order to live out my calling both as a pastor and a human being.

Job Descriptions

Many of you will remember the conversation crafted by Lewis Carroll between Alice (of Wonderland fame) and the Cheshire Cat. The interchange takes place at a fork in the road, and Alice begins by asking:

"Would you tell me, please, which way I ought to go from here?"
"That depends a good deal on where you want to get to."
"I don't much care where –"
"Then it doesn't matter which way you go."

That one bit of wisdom is worth the price of the book.

I once heard a sermon (you have probably heard it too as we all tend to "borrow" great insights), and its continuing theme was this one thought: "The main thing is to keep the main thing the main thing." This exercise in seeming redundancy raises an important point.

What is the main thing? What is our job, really? That might seem to be an easy one to answer. I am a pastor, or a plumber, or a personnel manager. But too often we let ourselves off too easily by answering in terms of the title of our occupation rather than dealing with what we should be about at life's deepest level while carrying out that occupation.

It has been my pleasure to know more than a few people who seemed to have something very special going on as indicated by the way they carried out the responsibilities of their job. They came to whatever their task was with a different sense of purpose and even a joy that infiltrated everything, and which enlivened all those around them.

I want to suggest that they have asked and answered a more important question than just "What do I do?" They have dealt with what they were really about, and the answer that they received and continue to receive colors not only the way they go to work, whatever that work might be, it shapes the way they live.

I have seen the effects of this in the realm with which I am most familiar. It appears to me that too often in the church we don't know what our job really is, and the result is that we occupy ourselves with busy work to fill the empty hours or focus on statistics to prop up our sense of meaning. (I must be doing something right, as I have all these forms to fill out, at least the bills are paid, and our attendance is about what it was last year at this time.)

It is always appropriate for us to ask, "What are we about, really?" Thinking in terms of the Alice-Cheshire Cat conversation, before we can decide which road we ought to take, we might want to have a clear idea of where it is that we want to go.

The truth is I have met too many people who do not seem to have a clue. And I have seen churches that did not have a clue. The result is a continuous going through the motions without any real indication as to why. Decisions are hard to make because there is no real basis upon which to decide. We end up falling back on the familiar criteria: "Do we have enough money?" "Who will be upset?" or the even more deadly "Well, what have we always done before?"

When I was in the eighth grade, we learned about "inertia" in Science class. I still remember the definition that we had to be able to repeat for the test: "The tendency of a body in motion to remain in motion unless acted on by an outside force" or conversely "the tendency of a body at rest to remain at rest until acted upon by an outside force."

If we are not careful, inertia becomes the basic theological principle operating in our congregations and our living. It is just easier, it is just more comfortable, it is just safer to continue on the same path even though that continuation ceases to be beneficial. We need to ask what our job is. We need to ask and then we need to live out of that answer.

But, maybe we don't want to know. Maybe it is just easier to float along doing what we have always done and getting the same result, or less.

My experience is that we hesitate asking that question. Maybe it is because of the effort involved, or maybe we are worried about the answer. We certainly come up with all sorts of ways to avoid the issue, the most common of which is assuming that "everybody knows what we are supposed to be doing."

Years ago I was part of a conference-wide group set to gather for its semi-annual meeting. I had served on the group previously, but had been away from its deliberations for several years and wanted a sense of how things might have changed.

As the meeting began, I asked innocently enough what we were hoping to accomplish over the next two days. "Oh, we don't have time to tell you that. We know what we are supposed to accomplish," was the response, and truth be told, we did have a nicely printed agenda, but my evaluation of the next 48 hours was that, in fact, we had no clue what we were trying to accomplish with that agenda. We just went through the motions, which duplicated what had been done in previous gatherings of this same group, without any real sense of that toward which we were working.

Maybe we don't ask because any sort of conflict makes us nervous, and we don't want to know that the various members of the body don't agree on their answer to the question. This lack of clarity of course can lead to misunderstandings at best and serious divisions at worst. "Surely the pastor should have known that she was supposed to do that." Which is countered by someone else saying, "Why would she? As I see it, that's not her job at all." How do you know who is right if there is not a common understanding of where we are headed and why? How does a staff person decide what is a part of his job description and what is not? Without a common understanding of what your job really is, you are certain to disappoint somebody.

> "Would you tell me, please, which way I ought to go from here?"
> "That depends a good deal on where you want to get to."
> "I don't much care where –"
> "Then it doesn't matter which way you go."

But we are the church, and it does matter. It matters a lot.

Saying "No" To A Good Idea

I have come to believe that the hardest thing for a United Methodist to do is to say no to a good idea. I am sure that it is hard for other faith communities as well, but my experience is with "the people called Methodists."

As I get older, one of my regrets is the number of things I didn't write down. I have in my mental repertoire all sorts of wonderful thoughts that I have heard other people say or read that other people wrote, and I use them all the time because I realize their importance. A few of them I can attach to a name, but others' sources are lost in the vapor. That is sad because I would like to give credit where credit is due.

Such is the case with this description of our organizational life together. Whoever said or wrote it posited that in groups we function in one of four ways: connection, cooperation, coordination, or collaboration. That appealed to me on several levels, the first of which is the fact that I spent my early years in Southern Baptist Churches, and so I have a fascination with alliterative sermon points. Second, and more important is the fact that this description gives us a handle on the different ways we do things together and why we are effective and why we are not.

Connection is the most basic and the most simple. It takes place when we are all in the same organization. We are all doing different things, but there is no common theme. We are doing them in the same place as a part of the same body, but otherwise everyone is pretty much on their own.

Cooperation is the next step. Here we begin to work out ways to accomplish our different tasks without stepping on each others' toes. This mainly involves scheduling and facilities' use, and usually involves the introduction of a calendar.

Coordination implies that we work together on some things, but that is not the consistent manner of doing business. It is more the occasional pleasant coincidence when we notice that several of us are interested in the same thing.

Collaboration happens when the group as a whole knows where it is headed and marshals its various efforts in that direction.

Too often we find ourselves somewhere between Cooperation and Collaboration and we can muddle through in that position, but we are not nearly as effective an organization as we might be, as we are called to be.

For several years, I worked with the Healthy Church Initiative in our conference. It was my experience that usually the first thing a congregation needs to do is to decide on its job, its mission, something we have already talked about on another occasion. But then comes the hard part. Once they center in on what they hold to be most important (which requires greater effort than one might think), then begins the even harder task of making decisions in light of that chosen mission. "What do we need to add?" "What do we need to change?" Both of those can be hard questions. But even harder is "What needs to be let go?" "How do we best marshal our resources to carry out our mission?"

Many congregations, as a part of the HCI program, are asked to do a Mission Audit in which they go through every activity of the congregation asking whether or not it is helping them accomplish their mission, and again this is harder than one might think. What makes this hard is that most congregations over the years have started this or that program simply because it seemed like a good thing to do. And these programs were started without the benefit of the congregation's awareness of its central mission. As a result they were not designed with a central focus in mind and so they might not be as effective as they could be, or they do nothing at all to further that mission, if in fact that mission exists.

The difficulty is increased because people become attached to programs, making it hard to let those programs go, or to even make the changes necessary to align them more closely with the central mission of the church.

The United Methodist Church has as its mission "to create disciples for the transformation of the world." What would it mean to adopt that as the central focus of the congregation's work? What if that were the operating norm by which we decide how we do what we do and even what we don't do, and why do we have to decide at all?

We have to decide because it is a question of stewardship. Years ago while I was serving at First UMC of Austin, we adopted the following as a mission statement: "We are called to make the best use of every resource entrusted to us by God, in order to bring as many people as possible into a lasting, life-changing relationship with God through Christ Jesus." Note especially the phrase "best use of every resource entrusted to us by God."

The Pareto Principle was established centuries ago as an economic theory. Its use has been expanded to countless applications in management theory. It says basically that twenty percent of our effort will yield eighty percent of the result. Conversely eighty percent of our efforts yield only twenty percent of the result.

That reality needs to be considered in the life of any congregation. Looking at all that goes on, what are the things that are most effective in accomplishing our mission? What are the things that are not so effective? I am not suggesting that the latter be eliminated unless they are completely nonproductive. I am suggesting that the way they are carried out might be changed to make them more effective in the accomplishing of the mission. More importantly what I am pleading for is a congregational commitment that those "most effective" things, the 20%, must be done and must be done well. The responsibility for their being carried out is of primary importance. Then we can look at other things.

You see, we deal with several limited commodities: people's time, people's money, and people's energy. We are responsible for being good stewards of those resources. We cannot afford to drain away those resources on less than effective programs while the possibilities that would most impact the success of our mission go wanting.

Yes, I know this is hard, but the task before us is important.

Leadership Vs. Management

There are a lot of articles and books being written about leadership in the church. Many of them are excellent, but, to me at least, some of them miss the point. And they miss the point because they confuse leadership with management.

Another one of the ideas that has managed to remain with me, without my remembering its source, describes the difference this way. Management is determining the best way to get up the ladder. Leadership is making sure that the ladder is leaning against the right wall.

It does not matter in the long run how well you are doing what you are doing if you are doing the wrong thing. Or put another way, simply being effective at getting a task done is not nearly as important as being clear whether or not this is the task that you ought to be doing.

I have finally come to realize that my experience is not necessarily normative for the whole of western civilization, but maybe this bit of personal confession will help. I always have lots of things that I could and should be doing. What I have learned about myself is that, given the multiplicity of responsibilities before me, I will tend to choose the one that is the easiest or the most pleasant or the least demanding. If there is an unpleasant conversation that I need to have, I will find it very important to work on an upcoming sermon, even if the Sunday when it will be delivered is months away. If there is a hard decision that needs to be made, I am sure to find some paper work that needs filling out. I mean, who can fault you for getting things done ahead of time? There are always things to be done, and those endless lists offer me countless ways to avoid the pressing, needful, and more difficult things that have accumulated on my personal desk.

Enough confession. I have found some of this same behavior in many organizations, maybe especially the Church. We have so much "stuff" that needs doing, and if we are not careful, after a while it all can seem equally important. The lists are endless, and there is only so much time, money, or human capital available. Given those realities, it is so easy to pick those tasks which are the easiest to get done or are the least unpleasant.

Now what does all that have to do with the difference between management and leadership? Too often we slip into management mode, looking for ways to more effectively do the easiest of the tasks before us. But leadership often means picking the harder, but more important, task and guiding the group toward being most effective in what it is truly called to be.

For example, I am sure it is quite important that we have the right worship colors for the Christian year, but it is probably more important to deal with the human needs both inside our congregation or right outside our door. Leaders can make sure that both get done, but are clear that the latter takes precedence over the former.

Managers are important; they get things done. Leaders are more important. They give us direction, and ultimately, what we need most is direction.

Life Isn't A Bumper Sticker

I hate to break this to you, but life is not always simple. We want it to be. We crave a bumper sticker reality in which everything is clear and defined, where the road signs unambiguously guide us to the appropriate response to any given situation. Our problem is that often our choices are not between good and bad but between bad and not so bad, or even harder, good and better. How do we decide which to do?

There are at least several responses to this situation. The first is to create our own reality, the one we want, one where everything is clearly good or bad, and the characters either wear black hats or white hats. The problem with this approach is that you have to "shoehorn" it into the real world. "Their position," whatever it is, that we have chosen to designate as the evil side, may not always be as evil, nor is "our side" always as righteous as we would like it to be in order for it to fit into our world view. There are certainly absolutes, but too often we cement our positions with bracing which glosses over truths that we would rather ignore.

Another response is to work off the assumption that everything is in flux. There are no absolutes. Every situation is brand new and in making the appropriate decision, we have to reinvent the wheel every time. Sure, Grandma taught us differently, but what does Grandma know?

Of course both of these options are "straw men," and we know neither of them work. We decide using what we have been taught, but what we have been taught should always be under consideration and re-evaluation because any study of history indicates that some things that were taught were later found to be incorrect at best, and extremely harmfully self-serving at worst.

Years ago when I was in seminary at Duke Divinity, I was faced with writing yet another paper. The needed research led me down into the mustiness that was the deeper levels of the Duke library (yes, we actually looked up things in books rather than "Googling" it). There I stumbled across a book some 300 pages long published in the 1860's. It was a biblical defense of slavery, page after page utilizing proof texts justifying one human being owning another. I was stunned. Who could think that way? Who could use my Bible in that way? Obviously that experience has stayed with me, and continues to serve as a curb on my enthusiasm when I am enrobed in the certainty of the rightness of my position.

I know that, but I find it hard to let go of things to which I have held for so long. In fact I may "double down" on my position lashing out at those who disagree, not because of my certainty, but because of my uncertainty and fear of being wrong and where that would leave me.

We know a lot these days because of all the media sources available to us. In fact there is so much data out there we can pick and choose our sources, and we often do, choosing those that align with us. Maybe you don't, but I do. As an aside, the Bible is like that. There is so much information from so many writers dealing with so many different situations that if I look hard enough, I can find a book, or a chapter, or a verse, or maybe just part of a verse that strengthens the position that I have already chosen, one that usually requires the least bit of change on my part.

Which leads to a more basic need: humility. Hard as it is for me to believe, at times I may not have the whole picture, the whole truth. Difficult as it is for me to fathom I might be wrong. With that nagging possibility in front of me, I am, in my best moments, open to the world and its possibilities, open to re-evaluation of my positions, open to the possibility that I might have placed the black hats and the white hats on the wrong people. With that awareness I plod forward.

As I said at the beginning, life is not simple. It is hard work. It requires constant study, re-evaluation and humility, but that is what is necessary if we are to live and live fully.

13

Golf Lessons
(A Parable About Change)

I once heard someone say "Golf is not a matter of life and death; it is more important than that." I don't believe that; at least most of the time I don't believe that, but I have leaned some important life lessons playing this most frustrating of games.

I first picked up a golf club the spring of my Junior year in college. Southwestern University was a small campus with an even smaller nine hole course just east of the gym, dining hall, and girls' dorms which made getting a round in rather simple. A friend had a set of clubs that I eventually used more than he did.

I parred the second hole I played, giving me, for the first of many times, the illusion that I had the slightest clue what this game was about. In the many years since, there have been some highs and more lows, but I stayed at it because I love the game.

After my retirement I decided to give myself the gift of lessons. I had been playing the game all this time with only one formal lesson, a gift from a church staff. But now I had time. Now I could get serious. To be sure, I was clear that the Senior Tour was not an option. I had seen great players up close and personal and just that observation helped me to understand that golf was never going to be my day job. But lessons would help, I just knew it.

I know what I expected. The pro would look at my swing and make a few suggestions to tweak this or that, and soon I would be playing so much better, because after all I had been playing sports all my life and had been at least adequate at most of them (I had the ugly letter jackets from high school and college to prove it). My golf history included several good scores and one fantastic score which I remember fondly, although the memory fades since it happened some 25 years ago. No, I was clear, a little fix here and there and I would be off to the races.

That illusion lasted about five minutes. Myron, the teaching pro and a wonderfully gentle and patient man, asked me to take some swings while he taped them so that we could both see what we were working with and toward. I did as he asked. Then we looked at the tape.

Immediately I had my first lesson. You have no clue what your swing really looks like. You are not doing what you think that you are doing. One look at the screen and even I could tell that my feet were too close together. Think about it, The first thing you learn is that you are not even standing correctly, something as basic as that.

So began the basic reconstruction of my game, piece by piece, and with that came another lesson: simply because I learned something once did not mean that I would not have to relearn it time and time again. Without conscious effort I would slip back into old habits. Myron would patiently remind me, "I know you know better than that, but you are (insert one of many faults) again."

I also learned that I had to practice, I had to work at it. I had to concentrate on making these new moves a normal part of the way I approached the game.

And most disappointingly, it was not an overnight process. I didn't walk out of the first lesson and break 80 immediately. In fact I was still struggling after the first ten- lesson package was completed. I was playing better and I had some better understandings of what I was doing wrong, but the sub 80 round was in the distance yet. In fact for a time the game was harder because I was constantly struggling to incorporate the changes that were needed. That was a great disappointment to me. I wanted improvement in my game, and I wanted it quickly and easily. Keep all that in mind for the next few paragraphs.

The statistics for church turnaround efforts are daunting; something like 70% of them fail. My guess is that they fail for some of the above listed reasons. We enter the process thinking that we are really doing most things right and all that is needed is just a tweak here or there: repaint the class rooms, change the hymns to some that I know, or any of countless small fixes or adjustments. And surely most of them can be accomplished quickly without the need for us to make any personal adjustments in the way we do things. In most cases, none of these expectations can be met, and because they are not met, the turnaround falters, disappointing everyone involved, and worse, innoculating them against trying anything new for the next twenty years.

We need to be clearer at the beginning that what we are undertaking is probably going to be difficult. Change always is. We will have to work intentionally at that change because we are used to old nonproductive habits, habits that we do without giving them any thought at all. And change will take time.

I know one congregation who had some members who became frustrated because they had made some important but difficult changes in the fall. It was now after Christmas, and things had not immediately turned around. In fact it was almost a year later before statistics began to indicate the changes were taking effect.

From time to time I went back to see Myron. It would have been months since my last lesson and things were starting to get shaky swing-wise. I would make some swings that he would record and he would run the tape and remind me of what I had been taught, of the changes that we had made, and of how important they were.

Which brings me to another lesson. My game will never be permanently fixed. There is always something about which I will need to be reminded. If I am not careful, if I am not intentional, the old habits will slip back.

Here ends the parable.

The Cost Of Doing Business

She was about as old then as I am now, which of course to my much younger eyes made her seem ancient. She was head of the family business and was obviously used to making decisions and having those decisions followed without a great deal of questioning.

She walked into my office that day with a strong sense of purpose. This was not unusual. It was the way she always made her entrance.

The conversation began this way: "I want him fired."
"You want who fired?" I asked.
"I want Bill fired. He's not doing his job."

This came as a shock to me as it would have to everyone else on the staff. Contrary to her evaluation, Bill was quite industrious and on more than one occasion had gone far beyond the boundaries of his part-time job description.

I tried to explain this to my angry visitor, but she would not hear any of it. In fact she "upped the ante." "Either you fire him or I will leave the church and take my pledge with me."

This represented no small threat. No, there was nothing small about it. Hers was the largest pledge that our congregation received each year, and I had enough experience with her to have no doubt that she would do what she threatened. If she did, it would be costly to the congregation's finances, and let's just say that money was not in abundance. We certainly did not have to have monthly meetings to decide what to do with our surplus. In spite of all that, my response was a quick one, probably surprising her as much as it surprised me. "Do what you have to do, but Bill is a good employee, and I will not fire him." She and her pledge walked out the door, and that was the last time I talked to her.

It has been my experience that there are wonderful words of wisdom contained in the lyrics of country western songs. Years ago I was driving toward San Antonio and yet another meeting. I was scanning the radio dial trying to find a station that would not break up while driving through the hill country. Suddenly, a song on one of the stations offered such words of wisdom sung with the required nasal twang: "If you marry for money, you will earn every penny." I have no idea who the artist was, and less idea who wrote the words, but I am grateful to whoever they were because the wisdom contained therein has stayed with me, and more than once has come to mind during appropriate settings. "If you marry for money, you will earn every penny."

In truth I responded as I did because of an earlier experience. In a previous church there was one parishioner who was a difficult case. Ours was a brand new congregation struggling to reach some form of stability. This fellow and his wife were active participants, and we needed all the active participants we could get, but their participation came at some cost. That cost was an occasional outburst from this one individual, always accompanied by a threat to leave the church.

I did all I could do to keep the peace. I bit my tongue often enough to leave scars. I let things go that should have been called into question. But finally, there was one more outburst, one more threat, but this time it was something too important to let pass. I simply had to speak, and I did, as gently as I could. Their response: I had never liked them, that I had always been against them, and that I had never made any effort to get along with them.

I remembered that couple from another time and another congregation that day in the office. Certainly I knew that there was going to be a cost in what I was about to do. The church did not have a great deal of money, the loss of that pledge would be hard to make up, but the young man was a good employee. Furthermore, I knew from at least one past experience that it was only a matter of time. Sooner of later there would be another issue and then another after that. Eventually there would be another demand accompanied by yet another threat and I would be faced with the same choice and the same gnawing feeling in my stomach that something about this was not quite right, that I was allowing myself to be bought off, that I was just putting off the inevitable-if not this time, some time.

Anyone in church leadership positions, clergy or lay, has had "those" conversations:

> "If you don't quit preaching about (fill in the blank), I will take my membership and my pledge to the church across town."
> "If you want the building fund to get the major gift that it needs from me, you are going to have to change the plans for that new youth center into a parlor that the whole church can use."
> "I had planned to include the church in my will, but if *that* is what you are gong to do, well...."
> "You know I do a lot each year to help raise apportionments, and if you want to keep that happening...."

So what is our response? First of all, I would suggest that you check your position. Is it the appropriate one as nearly as you can prayerfully discern? If it is, then try to explain your side or the church's side of things to the individual making the offer/threat. If he or she continues with conditions that you believe unacceptable and/or counter to the plans and mission of the congregation, then your answer must be "no," and you have to be prepared to live with the consequences.

Is there a cost involved in such a response? Of course there is. The budget may get tighter. That needed building might not get built yet. Apportionments might not get paid this year.

But there is also a cost involved in the other response you might make to such a situation. If you base your decision or program on just this financial consideration, there is the cost of redoing a decision that the congregation has worked through just to suit one individual. There is the cost of alienating others because the plans that have been faithfully adopted by the community have been altered or otherwise derailed. There is the cost of the congregation learning that some members are more important than others. And there is the personal cost: the cost of knowing that you chose to avoid an important issue or a needed confrontation to protect the cash flow, the personal cost of a sense of the diminishment of your calling, the personal cost that you've sold out, that you have made a decision based solely on the money.

There is also the important question of whether or not you are doing the person making the offer/threat any favor at all by agreeing to the demands being made. You are allowing that individual to continue to trust in the fact that his or her accumulation of "stuff" makes him or her special, or at least more special. Surely there is an idolatry here that needs confronting, if for no other reason than to indicate that you do not recognize that power into which he or she has come to place so much trust.

We as pastors are called to more than just raising budgets. We are called to build up the Body of Christ. This certainly includes paying attention to all of that Body, not just those possessing the largest accumulation of legal tender. We are called to seek after the growth of the whole congregation, not just the wants and needs of one or two. We are finally called to witness to the Christian community about the most basic Christian values. We are called to speak to the idol that we as a society have made of our money. This we cannot do if our ministry is forever a weather vane indicating which way the money goes.

That is the theological reason. There is a practical reason. "If you marry for money, you will earn every penny"

Fishing With Uncle Joe

Joe and Marie Burnley were more than my uncle and aunt, they were my second parents. Marie was my mother's younger sister, and she and Joe lived near us and their home served as a refuge when things got too ugly at ours.

Marie was great, but I had a Mother, a Dad-not so much. Uncle Joe filled in that gap. It was Joe who took me out the day of my dad's funeral to let me vent and to let me cry.

Uncle Joe and Aunt Marie introduced me to fishing, and fishing was very important in my young life. When I get into something, I want to know as much about it as I can learn. So I read, and at that stage of my life what I read about was fishing. I lived for the next issue of "Field and Stream" or "Sports Afield." I didn't mind waiting at the barber shop because they had sports magazines filled with articles about fishing. I soaked information up like a sponge, and having soaked it up I wanted to talk about it…a lot.

One day we were fishing, and I launched into the latest thing that I had learned. Of course, all this time I was thrashing around in the boat making all sorts of noise so that any bass in his right mind (assuming bass have a right mind) had left the vicinity long before we could get close enough to cast our lures. Joe listened for a while and then offered this pearl of wisdom, "For someone who knows so much about fishing, you don't catch many fish."

Apparently it is not enough just to know something from reading about it. You also have to learn from doing and from not doing. You need to know where to cast, but you also need to know not to kick things around in an aluminum boat.

I would hope that I had learned that larger lesson, but if I did, I seem to forget from time to time. I have all this stored up knowledge that I can dispense at a moment's notice, but it is not nearly as effective as it might be were I to put it into actual practice.

I was talking church politics and structure with an old friend from a sister denomination, and he told me how they deal with issues in their system. He said they designate a committee to write a draft paper which is then presented to a legislative body that dutifully goes through each word in each line making changes that most can agree to, whereupon the body adopts the paper and puts it into a filing cabinet never to be looked at again.

I sometimes feel that way about our creeds, faith statements, and, to a lesser extent, legislation at Annual Conference. We work hard at getting them worded exactly right, and then we store them away after congratulating ourselves on our great theological work, thinking we have actually accomplished something even though we often never get around to living out their basic principles.

I think I read this in something Bishop William Willimon wrote. He recounted a conversation with a lay person about the pastor's preaching at that individual's church. The man reported favorably, "The man scalds us every Sunday." But then after pausing he added thoughtfully, "but you know, we never change."

I wish I could finally learn what Joe tried to teach me so many years ago. It is not enough to just intellectually know. Somehow you have got to put what you know, what you hope you believe, into practice. That is, after all, where the real learning takes place.

We Are Doing This So That...

It was an afternoon session of a clergy enrichment group gathering sponsored by the Texas Methodist Foundation, where for two days a small group of us had the opportunity to pick the brain of Dr. Lovette Weems who heads up the G. Douglas Center for Church Leadership at Wesley Seminary in Washington, D.C. Dr. Weems has as his passion more effective church leadership.

I believe the general topic for that session was planning when he introduced a thought which went something like this. "As you are planning, try to summarize what you are hoping to accomplish in one sentence and then add these words to the end of that summary: 'so that...'"

He said that we always need to be able to complete the "so that" statement. We are doing whatever it is that we plan to do "so that...." In other words, we need to have a vision in mind as to why this event or this action should take place, to what end does it serve.

He told of being in a large meeting of Religious Education professionals, and to that gathered body he posed this question: "We are having Vacation Bible School this summer so that...," and he invited them to fill in the blank. He said the room went uncomfortably silent. Finally someone bravely volunteered a truth too often the case: "We are having Vacation Bible School this summer so that we can have Vacation Bible School." As I remember, he looked at us and said, "That is not enough of a reason."

Too much of what we do is not as effective as it might be because we have not thought through what it is that we really want to accomplish by doing it. Take the aforementioned example of Vacation Bible School. I would agree with Weems' suggestion that the purpose in mind for the event shapes how the event is carried out. If our purpose is to have the event because we have always had it and people expect it, then it will look one way and it might even appear very successfully done.

But what if this event was viewed as a part of the larger intent of the congregation to reach families not attending church or to move occasionally attending families into a deeper relationship. The programming might look the same, but the publicity in the surrounding area might be handled differently. Intentional efforts might be made to greet and to make new children to the group feel especially included. The parents who drop them off might be engaged in conversation. Follow-up letters might be sent saying how glad you were to see these children and, by the way, here are some future events especially for families that might be of interest. A call from the individuals who would be their Sunday School teachers might be in order. There are all sorts of possibilities, but they will only be dreamed and then carried out if there is first the awareness of why this event is being done in the first place.

Of course this applies to much more than just VBS. It applies to more than just church. It applies to all of life. Knowing why we are doing what we are doing informs how we do what we do, and if the "so that" exercise is not considered, the results of what we do will be less than they might have otherwise been

Everything Will Be Fine If We wake Up Tomorrow And It's 1955

Lyle Schaller died several months ago. His books and his very person were important parts of my growth in ministry. I first met him at a District Preachers' meeting in 1975. I was struggling with an issue at the time, and I cornered him during a lunch break asking for his assistance. He offered it, but as was often the case over the years, either through his books or his lectures, his answer was not what I might have expected, and that was good.

I last saw him as several of us pastors dropped him at the Austin Airport after he had met with our churches and with us personally for several days. He was a prolific writer and people buying his books, myself included, must have been a continuing encouragement for him because he kept at it for well over forty years.

I can't remember if I heard him say it or read it in one of his books (it might have been both as he tended to repeat himself, repetition being the soul of pedagogy), but this is one of his many thoughts that have stuck with me. "Everything will be fine if we wake up tomorrow and it's 1955."

Some of us who are older remember 1955 as a time when churches were full and membership was an expected part of the social fabric. We remember when everything was closed on Sunday because it was the sabbath (except for the cafeteria where we all ate after church, but that didn't seem to bother anyone). There were no children's athletics events on Sunday morning. There was nothing to do but church which may explain why we did as well as we did. We remember a time when it seemed the churches were centers of community life. A pastor friend of mine and I were talking before he died. He recalled successfully starting a congregation in the late fifties and how easy it was to grow it to over a thousand members. He said that basically all you had to do was open the doors on Sunday morning. We remember all that and more, and we wish it could be that easy for us again, but it is not.

But before you pine too much for a return to the 50's, you need to remember that all was not "peaches and cream" during that time. The good times were not evenly distributed. Jim Crow still held sway. Many schools were separate and not even close to equal. It was a time of fear and suspicion. Any one different from you was probably a communist. And church was comfortable, maybe too comfortable in many places. And we loved our comfort so much that when challenges of race or gender or anything else that mattered came forth, too often we spent time combing the scriptures to find justification for our "entrenched-ness." It was too easy to divide up the population into "us" and "them." We seem to forget a lot of that, those of us who lived through those years. And forgetting, we might then want to go back. In fact, I am hearing many of the same discussions using the same arguments now that I heard then, only the subjects of the disagreements have changed.

It is true that it requires more effort now to be the church. We are less and less at the center of things, and that might not be all that bad. At times in the past, we struggled so hard to stay at the center that we may have given up our souls to remain in that place of privilege.

We need to face some hard questions about what it means to be the Church in the year 2016. What does it mean to be faithful in the midst of a severely divided society? How do we speak to the inequality that exists? What is our responsibility to the poor;? What about those who have been pushed to the edge by the way we do things, by the self-interested way we see things. My reading of recent history and my experience over the years indicates that these are not new questions.

It is not 1955 and in so many ways, that is a good thing. It seems harder now to be the church, but I wonder if it really is. I believe that it has always been difficult to be faithful and to live out the call of the one we claim to follow. That was true in 1955 and equally true some sixty years later.

A Needed Loss Of Certainty

At times I miss the certainty of my youth. I have told countless groups that I never was smarter than when I was sixteen years old. Then I was absolutely clear on the categories. I knew what was right and wrong. I knew who wore the black hats and who wore the white ones.

It has become a bit foggier since. Some in the black hat category have turned out to have some redeeming qualities, while the white hats have demonstrated some serious flaws. There have been too many occasions where the options were not good and bad, but good and better, if I was lucky, or bad and not so bad if I was not.

Gradually it has become clearer and clearer to me that things are not always so clear.

I was introduced to Harry Chapin in the early 1970's. I was pastoring two small churches outside of San Angelo. Their location necessitated some serious driving time, and there was only one radio station that I could pick up. At that time KGKL from Angelo was not what I wanted to listen to, so I was in search of something to break up the monotony of the drive. Enter the eight track tape player. A friend helped me install one in my car, and I was set. My musical library consisted of mainly Jim Croce and Harry Chapin, both singer/song writers, and most importantly to me, story tellers. Hearing their stories, I gained significant truths for my life. (Which by the way is the best reason for stories.)

I especially liked Harry Chapin. I especially learned from Harry Chapin. The words from his song "There Was Only One Choice" have stayed with me.

It' s not enough to listen…it's not enough to see..
When the hurricane is coming on, it's not enough to flee
It's not enough to be in love…we hide behind that word
It's not enough to be alive when your future's been deferred

What I've run through my body, what I've run through my mind
My breath's the only rhythm…and the tempo is my time
My enemy is hopelessness…my ally's honest doubt
The answer is a question that I never will find out"

In retrospect, I am not as enamored with certainty as I once was. It is probably because way too often I have been wrong, or short-sighted, or blind to possibilities because I already knew the answer. Sixteen was nice, but I would just as soon not go back. Of that I am almost certain.

Prayer On An "As Needed" Basis

It was a tradition in our fraternity house that grace was offered before meals. On occasions that was quite interesting given the theological bent, or lack thereof, of many of the young men living there.

One day in particular comes to mind. It was lunch time and we were nearing the end of finals week. When called upon to offer grace, the designated "pray-er" for the meal offered this, which probably will not make it into the Book of Common Prayer. "Dear God, we need help. Give us help. Amen." Not a bad prayer if you think about it, but what made it memorable was the grace offered at supper that night. It was offered by the same fellow, but now his finals were over. He prayed these words. "Dear God, we don't need help anymore. Forget it. Amen."

The second prayer is what makes the event stick in my mind over 50 years later. It sticks because it is so typical of our relationship to God. We want God there in the hard times, but when things get straightened out, we believe that we can handle it from here on, or at least until the next crisis arises.

Strangely enough, it reminds me of some political history in our country and particularly in our state. The Depression era was brutal on the lives of just about everyone. There seemed no way out for so many people, and in truth, left on their own, there probably wasn't. The government stepped in and through all sorts of programs gave people jobs and ways to get by. And people were grateful…for a while. But then they got back on their feet and they and their children, whose memories of the breadlines and no work were a little vague, began to believe that government had no place. They seemed to forget those direly needed actions that had been taken on their behalf or on behalf of their parents and grandparents. Suddenly government helping people was not right. I am back on my feet. I have got mine. Leave me alone. Those other people can take care of themselves.

It is probably just in my mind, but there seems to be a connection here, and if there is, we need to maintain a memory, it seems to me.

Ann Lamott writes these words in her book Help, Thanks, Wow:

"Prayer is talking to something or anything with which we seek union, even if we are bitter or insane or broken. (In fact, these are probably the best possible conditions under which to pray.) Prayer is taking a chance that against all odds and past history, we are loved and chosen, and we do not have to get it together before we show up. The opposite may be true: We may not be able to get it together until after we show up in such miserable shape."

Back to what I see as the problem. We get in touch with that which is at the center of things in the midst of our brokenness, but then on the other side of the pain we tend to forget that connection. Finals are over. We don't need help anymore, and that connection just established which could continue to enrich our lives and the lives of those around us, slides away because of the mistaken belief that now we can handle it ourselves. Just a brief review of history, both personal and larger, would indicate that is most likely not the case.

Neighbor? Which Neighbor? Who is My Neighbor?

Let's begin with an incredibly uncomfortable text. Now it might not seem that way on the surface, but the smallest amount of thought will lead you to understand that something is going on here that, at best, will make us all uncomfortable.

Romans 13:8-10 New International Version

> Let no debt remain outstanding, except the continuing debt to love one another, for whoever loves others has fulfilled the law. The commandments, "You shall not commit adultery," "You shall not murder," "You shall not steal," "You shall not covet," and whatever other command there may be, are summed up in this one command: "Love your neighbor as yourself." Love does no harm to a neighbor. Therefore love is the fulfillment of the law.

For me there are two very attention-grabbing words here-love and neighbor. I begin with love. My college and seminary years happened while the debate between Christian Ethicists Paul Ramsey and Joseph Fletcher was going on. Ramsey was a rule guy. His basic question was "what is the rule?" Fletcher was a love guy. "Which option facing us produces the most love?" (I admit that this reduces both of them to caricatures, and for that I apologize.) This discussion was of course taking place in the late sixties, when we were struggling with the fact that some of the rules that we had accepted might have been put in place for just our benefit to the detriment of some others.

While at Duke I took several courses from Dr. Waldo Beach who chose a middle path between the two. (I think he was Presbyterian but he would have made a great Methodist.) He thought it was important to consider the rules, but they have to be considered in light of the greater claim to love.

Of course you could spend hours and pages defining love. In fact, one of the critics said something like "love slips through Fletcher's pages like a greased pig." And defining love can be tough, especially with hundreds of "moon-June" lyrics from our childhood upon which to draw.

We have all heard the sermon which highlights the fact that there are three different Greek words, all of which we English speakers translate as love even though their meanings are very different. I understand there may be more shades of meaning than that in the Hebrew. For our purposes here, I would opt for "unconditional positive regard" as a place to start. God loves us unconditionally. That which is at the center of things views us positively, and hopes for the same from us. That seems to fit with "love your neighbor as God has loved us." But then with even that broad definition, we run into trouble when we begin to talk about the neighbor.

There was a religious lawyer attempting to work his way out of this dilemma of loving the neighbor, and he asked the question of Jesus that we would like to ask. "Exactly who is my neighbor? Where can I draw the line? Surely there are some people that I am not supposed to love. That line about love does not harm; surely that does not apply universally. I mean, there are people who have hurt me. There are people who have different political beliefs than I have. They have said some horrible things to me and about me. Their religion is different than mine. Surely I only have to love those who are like me, who think like I think, who believe what I believe, who hate the same people I hate, who love me first. There have to be some limits to this love business, and if there aren't, then there certainly should be."

This text is hard because there are no footnotes or provisos. It is such a sweeping statement, and Jesus' telling that story about the Good Samaritan in answer to the squirming lawyer is certainly no help. A Samaritan, really?

We have invested great effort in deciding who is deserving of our love. We have combed the scriptures for justifications for our delineations. We have carefully chosen what we watch and what we read in order to get to a place of comfort in our separateness. Then we are confronted with Jesus, and we either have to bend ourselves, or more likely we bend our view of Jesus, into pretzels in order to remain comfortable where we are.

I wish I were just talking about you. I really do. But the truth is I am talking about me, I am talking about us, and the distance between us and Jesus and how far we have to travel to get home.

The older I get, the clearer it becomes. Love is hard. Loving others as God has loved us is at most times extremely difficult, but it is important. It is important because it is the center of our life together. It is how we are created to live.

Altar Calls

I have been to more than a few revivals in my life. One remains locked in my memory because of the altar call on the last evening. The services were taking place in a small town in North Carolina, and the preacher posed the question in this way: "What if you are killed in a car wreck going home, and you did not come forward? Where will you spend eternity?"

I have to say that I have a number of problems with that approach theologically. For one thing, I do not like what it says about God, who I believe to be loving. Would God separate himself or herself from someone for eternity because of a missed altar call?

Now, does that mean that altar calls are not important? No, it certainly does not. Does it mean that alter calls only happen at the end of revivals? Again, no, it does not.

For me there are numerous altar calls, points in our lives where decisions are made, life changing decisions. There are those times when we decide to reorient our lives, to re-center ourselves around something that matters rather than the trivialities that so often consume us. And after that, to the extent that those decisions are lived out, our very living is different. So altar calls matter, and they happen a lot more often that you would like to think.

I believe it was Senator Howard Baker, in the Watergate hearings so many years ago, who first put the question which has been used so often since. He asked "What did you know and when did you know it?"

I want to pose a slightly different form of that question. "What are you going to do and when are you going to do it?"

I think we have a sense that things aren't working. We feel that, and we would really like to find someone or something to blame for it. In response to that need a whole industry has grown up to point us toward this or that as the whole reason for things being the way that they are. Not surprisingly, the ones that are most popular shift all the blame outward and leave us completely without fault.

But what if the problem starts closer to home, and I mean a whole lot closer to home? What if it is closer than the person sitting next to you in the pew? What if the person you look at in the mirror every morning is at least partially responsible? What if I have to come to grips with the fact that at least a significant part of the problem is me and the decisions that I have made, the things I have chosen to value? What if the scriptures are right? What if love really is at the center of things-love, not power, not money, not position? I think deep down we know the truth. And to the extent that we admit that, to that extent we are aware of a need for change.

That would bring us, you and me, to my question: "So what are you going to do, and when are you going to do it?"

Dr. Dudley Steinspring was a professor at Duke Divinity School. It fell to him to try to teach me Hebrew, a task made harder by the fact that since I had grown up in South Texas, I assumed every language that was not English should be pronounced with a Spanish accent. The looks on his face when I tried to read spoke volumes.

Dr. Steinspring had been teaching Hebrew for years, and he had developed numerous techniques to explain the differences between that language and English. One of those differences had to do with accent patterns. Apparently there are two dominant patterns. I can only remember one. He told us that the phrase "begin now" was the same as one of the dominant patterns. So whenever we pronounced the sounds of a word correctly, but not that accent pattern, he would say, "Remember, begin now."

I know our usual response to important decisions. It is to say "Well, not just now. There will be other chances." I know because I resemble that remark. What I am saying is now matters.

I am not saying decide now so that in case you are in a car wreck going home you will be on the right side of the heavenly ledger. I am saying decide now so that this moment and the ones following it will be different; so that the rest of this day will be different; so tomorrow will be different, and the day after that and the day after that; so that your relationships will be different; so that your world view will be different; so that your life is richer, not financially in spite of what the prosperity preachers will tell you, but richer and fuller because you live more in the awareness of God now and every moment to come. That, by the way, is the way you were created to live, and every moment you and I do not so live, our lives are less. Now matters.

Will you backslide? Absolutely. It is a hard world in which to keep faith. From time to time, maybe even moment to moment, you will need another altar call, a reminder, a booster shot if you will.

Will you need re-enforcement through worship? Certainly. We all gather as resident members of "backsliders anonymous", and we say through our corporate prayers of confession "I am John, and I am a backslider." and all those around us affirm they are in the same circumstance. But we strengthen each other today and always. We strengthen each other to make again that important choice about who we will choose to follow and to live out that life-giving option.

So take a look. How's it going, really? Before you start looking around for some one or something to blame, take a look at yourself. Certainly there are occasions when others do things that mess things up for us. For sure the conditions around us make life harder than it needs to be. But most often we can't control all those factors. However, there is one factor that we can control. There is one factor for which we are responsible. We can do our part to heal relationships out of love. We can re-center ourselves around that which really matters. We can start there, wherever that is.

So in the face of this hour and all the hours before it, in light of the scriptures and what we have come to know about life, and based on our perception of God in our lives, the question arises. What are we going to do and when are we going to do it?

Dr. Steinspring would suggest that you "Begin now."

Good Words Lost

Over the years something has become more and more clear to me. We often throw around terms in our conversations acting as though we all know what they mean, and for which we assume we all have a common definition.

And this is another of those occasions where we never ask. Maybe we don't want others to know what we don't know. Maybe our fear is that we are the only ones in the room with just a vague clue of what is being discussed. So we nod our heads and make the appropriate sounds at the appropriate times (we hope).

But after sitting through a lot of these discussions over the years, I am convinced that too often too many of us have widely varying definitions for the same terms. This means that in many of our conversations we are like ships passing in the night.

One result of our cooperative vagueness is that we allow good words to slip out of our vocabulary because we don't agree necessarily with what we think they mean, or it sounds like something a rival denomination might say, and Lord knows, we don't want to be confused with them.

In my own tribe, the people called Methodists, some of us have slowly eased out the word "saved." Why is that? Maybe it is because we have accepted a definition that fits someone else's theology which differs from our own, and so we have jettisoned it from our conversations. I believe that to the extent we have done that, we have not only diminished our theological vocabulary, we have lost sight of at least a portion of that which is offered us by a loving God.

Maybe we don't want to think about the fact that our lives could stand some "saving." Maybe we would like to believe that indeed all is "well with my soul," when a realistic appraisal might indicate otherwise.

Ann Lamott in <u>Stiches</u> offers this definition:

> "When we agree to (or get tricked into) being part of something bigger than our own wired, fixated minds, we are saved."

Here "saved" means something else than just getting your ticket punched into heaven. It means a re-centering of ourselves around something other than ourselves. It means having something other than ourselves for which to live. It means seeing everything from a different perspective. It is a way of talking about conversion (metanoia in the Greek) which translated means "to turn around." In turning around, our lives are given back to us. Our living is literally saved. It is what the faith is about.

But "we" don't use that word because we might sound like "them," whoever "them" happens to be. The sad thing is that we might still be able to use that particular word and so many others had we taken the time to talk with each other about what they might mean for us, rather than just deleting them from the conversation because we don't want to show our ignorance, or be confused with someone else and their definitions.

The Importance Of Vision

Let's begin with two quotes that at first seem unrelated The people making them certainly are.

The first comes from Phil Jackson, a pro basketball player who became a successful coach (probably helped some by coaching some guy named Jordon) and who is now managing the New York Knicks. He wrote

"You cannot be what you cannot see."

The second quote comes from Lily Tomlin, the comedienne who rose to fame on "Rowan and Martin's Laugh In" (a formative experience for those of us old enough to remember it). She said,

"I always wanted to be somebody, but I guess I should have been more specific."

As one who has long been frustrated by the game of golf, I spend more than a bit of time reading about the game hoping against hope that I will find that one tip that will transform my consistent experience of mediocrity into something a bit more acceptable.

One of the things that I have learned is that golf is not just a physical exercise, it is a mental one as well. Numerous writers have pointed out that central to that reality is the need to have in mind what you want the shot you are about to hit to look like. It is not enough to utter the usual golfer's prayer, "Please, hit this out of the sound of laughter." It is not enough to say to yourself, "I just want to hit the fairway." You have to be very specific as to what you want to accomplish. You are not just aiming at the fairway, you are aiming at the tree just to the right of the green. The idea is that the more focused you are, the clearer you are about what you want to get done, the more likely you are to be successful. And even if you are just a little off, you will be in better shape because you have been clear about what you specifically wanted to accomplish. The theory is that your body will react to a specific plan more effectively that just a generalized hope.

So what is your vision for today? What do you want to specifically accomplish? If your only vision for the next few hours is to make it through the next few hours, you probably will accomplish that, but most likely there is more that could have happened.

If you are clear about what you want to accomplish, there is a greater possibility that you will make progress in that direction because you will make decisions based on that vision. I think Jackson is right. "You cannot be what you cannot see." But I also think Tomlin is right in seeking a bit more specificity.

A Better Christian Than You

Everybody has to have somebody to look down on,
Who they can be better than at anytime they choose,
Someone doing something dirty decent folks can frown on.
If you can't find somebody else, then help yourself to me.
     Kris Kristofferson, "Jesus Was a Capricorn"

I first heard this song in the early 70's driving somewhere between Mertzon and Christoval, Texas. It was true then in that troubled time. It is true now. Only the names have been changed, and few of us are innocent.

There is an old joke/parable about two men confronting a bear. One fellow yells for them to run. As they are trying to get away, the other fellow says between gasps," We can't outrun this bear," to which the first man says, "I don't have to outrun the bear. I just have to outrun you!"

As I look across the theological and political spectrum these days, (and it is harder and harder to tell them apart) and as I listen to members of the faith eager to define those who are Christian and those who aren't, this oft-told tale comes to mind. How many times have we heard someone say, "I don't even think that person is a Christian?" Usually that means that person holds a different opinion than mine, is more liberal or conservative than I am, or has upset me in some other way.

But maybe there is more to it than that. Maybe we are operating on the "outrun you" principle. I may not be all that great religiously, but I am certainly better than you, and we all know that God grades on the curve.

Or maybe we know that deep down we have some uncertainties, and those who differ with us raise issues which we would rather not deal with at all. That being the case, it is just easier to discount them and their faith rather than to struggle with the possibility that something about us or our ideas might not be perfectly in line and thus might need to be changed.

Something I heard years ago has stuck with me. "I have never heard of a religion that believed that everyone was going to heaven but us." Usually we define the categories so that we come out ahead. "Their" sins are unforgivable. "Mine" are not nearly so serious in the great scheme of things.

It was a hard thing for me to learn, but I don't know everything, and at the risk of making myself the norm for western civilization, I wonder if any of us do. Going even further out on this limb, I would posit that one of the main needs of the faith community is a sense of humility. We act as if we know beyond a shadow of a doubt everything there is to know about God. My experience tells me that is not the case, that God is larger than we are and too many of our definitions are limits on God and ways of making ourselves feel better about ourselves, especially in relationship to those around us.

I had a good friend who was the "world's foremost authority." (I trust you know someone like this.) He was seemingly certain of his opinion on just about any subject. One day after listening for a while, I said, nicely, "It must be a terrible responsibility to know everything." Without hesitation he answered, "Yes, it is." Of course we both knew the truth. Neither of us knew everything but at times we act like we do, and we deal with others like that is the case.

There are many facets to faith, but to me one of the most important is humility. We do not know everything. I haven't even figured out how my cell phone works. How does that signal find me whether I am in Austin or at the lake or wherever? If I can't fathom that, certainly all that God is, is be beyond me. That's why we study. That's why we worship. That's why we pray. We are constantly seeking more understanding of that which is at the center of things. Why? Because we need it. We are still looking for the whole truth, the full story. That is something to remember when we attempt to place ourselves ahead in the line.

We can always find "someone to look down on, who we can be better than at any time we choose," But there is more to our relationship with God than an "outrun you" theology

Ministry As A Shared Reality

Too often pastors and congregations enter into an unhealthy agreement. The pastor decides to do all the ministry and the congregation decides to let him or her do just that. This is harmful on a number of levels. So why does it happen?

It begins with the pastor not being clear on his or her job description. As mentioned on other occasions, we are not clear about what we should be about, and as a result we try to do everything that comes up. And we do so for any number of reasons: we want people to think that we are competent. We want to meet their expectations even though no one is really clear what those expectations are, and we want people to think that we are special.

A generation or so ago we began to professionalize ministry. This was a good thing in that people were equipped with skills needed to serve, but a strange thing happened. A "leave it to the professionals" attitude developed in our congregations. After all, those people are trained to be "ministers." Lay people thought they couldn't visit the sick because they had not had the training in pastoral care that had been afforded their pastor. They could not teach because they had not had theological training in seminary. They could not witness because they missed out on the preaching classes that their pastors had received. All that is best left to the professionals.

This worked out well for everyone, it seemed. Pastors were made to feel more special and lay persons were relieved of responsibility to actually be the church. But a problem developed because neither party was actually doing what needed to be done for the benefit of everyone concerned.

Here's the problem: people need to be in ministry in order for their faith to grow. This is not just an intellectual enterprise. The faith must be lived out, and to the extent that people handed over ministry to the professionals, they lost the opportunity for their faith to grow.

This is not a new thought with me certainly, but it needs to be said from time to time so that we don't lose track. The function of pastors is to enable people to do ministry. At least one function of worship is to encourage the participants to more fully participate in ministry: to be with those who are hurting, to teach, to be in ministry with the poor. Pastors should utilize their training by training others to be more effective in their witness. People can be taught to be more helpful in hospital visitation and other settings. (Stephen Ministries comes to mind.) Pastors can teach with the intention that those participating can then move on to teach others.

Effective congregations multiply their resources. Truly effective pastors equip the laity to do ministry. Laity in ministry find their faith enhanced. The "lone wolf" pastor who tries to do it all also faces the problem of burnout because there is just more to do than any one person can handle. The congregation who lets, or worse expects, their pastor to "do it all" costs themselves the opportunity to grow in their faith through individual acts of ministry.

The "It's All Right" People

As I look back over the years of my ministry, it is clear to me that I was blessed in almost every congregation with "it's all right people." In most cases they were older and more experienced than I was. They had a real sense of what it means to be "church." They had a history of holding responsible positions in the church, and they were generally respected throughout the congregation. They wanted the best for the church and they wanted the best for me, and they saw those two as being linked.

Over the years I learned to recognize these people and to talk with them about the needs of the church. I would share my ideas and dreams with them. Because of the relationship that we had developed they could ask me questions or raise issues that they saw with the direction I was describing. When I was at my wisest, I would stay with the conversation until I had answered their questions, or until they convinced me that mine was not the best option at that particular time. There was always benefit from those conversations.

But there was an added benefit. Because these individuals were trusted by the congregation, other people who had concerns about a particular direction or program would come to them expressing concern. And because of our conversations, these individuals could explain where we were going and why. They could also assure people that the idea had been given some thought. In summary their conversation would sound like this: "What is John doing?" Answer: "We have talked about it, I understand it, and it's all right." The questioner did not have to trust me totally because he totally trusted the person to whom he was talking.

So, if you would, allow me to offer a word of council, first to pastors. Find someone who has a real sense of the faith and the best interests of the congregation at heart and talk with them regularly. Share with them your hopes and dreams and take seriously their responses. Second, to laity, be open to fulfilling the role of the "it's all right person." The value of people who can say that they know what is going on, who can say that there are good possibilities within an idea, is hard to overestimate. They can save a pastorate and they can save the ministry of a congregation. In our internet-cable TV world, we have become too good at being critics and less able to build each other up.

In every congregation I have served I can list the names of the people who helped save my ministry, and I thank God for the "it's all right people."

Survival Is Not Mandatory

It is a meme that I have shared from time to time in presentations I have made. What you notice first is the picture of an intact skeleton of a dinosaur. With that grabbing your attention, you then notice the words; "It is not necessary to change. Survival is not mandatory."

It is a hard thing to accept at times, but change is continually going on around us. Harder to accept is the fact that change is continually going on *within* us. We like to think of ourselves as stable rocks in the midst of things, but as I get older I am more and more aware of how things have changed in my lifetime, and how I have changed in that same period.

I have seen the pendulum of history swing back and forth between liberal and conservative in politics and in the church (although at times i have to admit that there is so little difference between the two). I have seen changes within myself as certainty was replaced by humility, a process made necessary by the happenings of the world around me. I have seen things that went along unquestioned for years be challenged and changed, however painfully.

And I have watched the church struggle against change. It might be over liturgy or music. It has been, and continues to be, struggles over any number of social issues, notably abortion and sexuality. It might be over structure. It often boils down to a struggle over who gets to call the shots.

Years ago a now departed friend of mine, John Gibbs, said this, "Every time I get into a position to take advantage of the system, someone changes the rules." When he said that, I assumed he was talking about delegate elections for our General Conference (and he probably was), but the truth of what he said carries so much further than that.

Pastors, and many others, got to where they are by doing things a certain way, and to the extent that they have been successful, they tend to assume that everyone will do well if they do things exactly that way. That disregards at least two things.

First, not every situation is the same. All churches do have some similarities, but they also are unique. That being the case, a "one size fits all" approach is not necessarily effective in all situations.

Second, the world has changed somewhat over the years. What worked ten years ago might not be nearly so effective now. And we know that, at least to some extent, but we have a tendency to hold on to what we have known because that got us where we are. We know that worked, and we stick to it even though it might not be as effective as it used to be, if effective at all.

Now there is, of course, another danger, and that is that we can jump on to every change that comes along. Again, one of the benefits of being my age is having seen the fads that have come and gone, many of which I was convinced promised the complete salvation of the church. As I said, most of those came and went, and we are where we are…still.

So, this is another place where leadership is important, and leadership is difficult. We are constantly on a tightrope trying to balance those things that need to be kept in place and those things that need to be changed. Just because it got us where we are does not make it better for all of creation. It may be that our only hope is to be clear as to where we are finally headed and to focus on that, rather than our attachment to what got us here and the attractiveness of whatever new trinket of an idea just came along.

A Marathon, Not A Sprint

When I was in high school in my relatively small town, we all played several sports. (Obviously this was before the age of specialization which is the dominant modus operandi today.) That meant that, come spring, we ran track. Now let me pause here to say that I am not now nor have I ever been fleet of foot. Needless to say that put me at a bit of a disadvantage in that particular sport.

When the season began, the coach determined that I should run the quarter mile, and that's what I did while also training for the long jump on the side. One day while practicing the long jump, I pulled a muscle due to a lack of sufficient warm up. This happened on a Tuesday and we had a meet on Saturday. It was decided that I had to run something, but the quarter mile would have demanded more speed than I could muster. The answer: move me to the half mile. And so it was I found myself walking to the starting line for that distance, never having raced at that distance before. I asked the coach what my strategy should be. He looked at me with a rather strange expression and answered, "Gut it." And that is exactly what I did. I started out like I had previously run quarter miles. The good news was that at the end of the first lap I was seventh. The bad news was that I had already "hit the wall" a quarter lap back. What followed was one of the longest laps I ever ran and the humiliation of finishing dead last by a mile. From then on I had a new strategy. Don't finish last. For the next few races I would hang back and then try to be sure I could pick off the last of my fellow stragglers.

Years later, in my mid thirties, I started running again. And after several months of training, I decided to enter a ten K run that was being held nearby. I still had a memory of my running in high school and so I planned out how I would run the course. I would run ten-minute miles which seemed like a good pace given my training and experience. I was comfortable at that pace, and I thought that would get me through. I just wanted to finish and, more importantly, not finish last.

The run began, and I was moving along quite comfortably I thought. The shock came when I arrived at the end of the first mile. There was a gentleman there with a stop watch counting off the time. As I neared him, I could hear him counting off, "57, 58, 59." Fine, I thought, right on target, but that thought disappeared with his next words: "Eight minutes." I had gone out way too fast, and the end of the run was on a slight uphill. I finished the run in just over an hour, but what a long and humbling hour. At one point a lady (She must have been 40 years my senior) jogged past me and waved.. But that was not the worst moment. That came when I was passed by a lady walking her cocker spaniel.

The lesson in all of this: "Life is a marathon, not a sprint." It is about endurance, not just occasional bursts of speed that look good but drain you for the ongoing run.

We tend to enter new situations, new jobs, new relationships, eager to impress, and so we hit the ground running, which is all well and good if it is a manageable pace that can be sustained. But too often we run a far-too-fast first lap or mile raising others' expectations, as well as our own, while draining ourselves of resources that will be needed over the long haul.

For me an eight minute mile at that stage was great speed, but it was disastrous for the rest of the run. Great starts can indeed be great, but they may sap you for the long haul, and it is the long haul that matters.

If I Had It To Do Over Again,
I Would Take A Day Off

I got to know Ted Richardson through my first boss, Darrell Gray. They were best friends and, as a result, I was introduced to "the Godfather," as I would come to refer to him. Ted had been a District Superintendent several times and was deeply involved in the politics of our conference. He was, and always had been, a hard charger. He had been a part of the church's wars with the John Birch Society, as well as all the struggles with the issues from war to integration to homosexuality that arose during the sixties. He had achieved a successful career. I came to view him as one of my sources for all sorts of practical information.

One day some twenty years into our relationship, I asked him what he would have done differently over the years. I don't know what I expected, but I was surprised by his answer, "I would take a day off."

Earlier I wrote about understanding life and ministry as a marathon, not a sprint, that we are in it for the long haul, whatever it is that we are hauling. We can go full tilt, twenty-four hours a day, but we won't last long before we are worn down to nothing.

Whatever our job, there is a need for designated time away to refresh ourselves, to renew ourselves. Early on I convinced myself that I would take my time off as it became available. The result of that decision was that I never really felt "away." There was always something that needed to be done that colored whatever I was doing with a shade of guilt. With some designated time away, I could say this is "my time." Those other everyday responsibilities will be there when I get back. I need some time to recover.

I also had activities and places that took me away. You would realize by now that one of those was golf. I was lucky enough to have a regular group that allowed conversation that mitigated the frustration that game brings. We were fortunate to be able to spend time at the lake where I had a shop. There I built simple furniture and other things. The planning and carrying out of those plans were a refreshment to my soul. Even clearing cedar from the property was helpful. You could see an immediate result, and the exercise was good for me. Whatever the activity, I came back to my job of pastoring refreshed and more capable of dealing with the various stresses of the job.

Now, of course, discipline is necessary. You can't be off all the time (even when you are retired). But there is importance in time away, an opportunity for rejuvenation. It is an investment in yourself and in the lives of all you touch. You bring a better self to the rest of your life when that self has some time away.

I listened to Ted on many subjects, but he was especially right on this one. If you want to have a full life, take a day off.

Farther Along

I am not sure why she came, but every Wednesday night she would come to the Bible study I was leading at the small west Texas congregation that I was serving. She was a member of another congregation which was certainly more conservative than was ours, and she was probably one of its more conservative members. But almost every Wednesday, there she was.

I was two years out of seminary and more certain about things religious than I probably ought to have been, and so more often than not there was some disagreement between us as to the meaning of the text that we were discussing.

There was one particular Wednesday getting nigh on to Christmas. The texts for discussion that evening were appropriate to the season. As I prepared for one particular session a thought came to mind. I had a way to catch her. You see, too often, our conversations devolved into a contest. At least they did from my end. When she walked in the door that night, I was ready. I let the conversation go on for a while, and then I set the trap. "Here is the problem," I said. "Jesus is either the product of a virgin birth or he is of the house and linage of David. Which is it?" There, I had her, her and her literal mindset. At least I thought I did. She paused only for a moment or two and then made this response which I have savored for 40 years. She looked me right in the eye and said, "Someday, we will know, John McMullen. Someday we will know."

Thinking back on that occasion, the words of the old hymn come to mind:

> "Farther along, we'll know all about it.
> Farther along we'll understand why.

Cheer up my brother.
Walk in the sunlight.
We'll understand it all by and by."

She was much older than I, and she was much wiser than I.

The older I get, the more certain I am of that which I don't know for sure; that there are some things that are beyond my pay grade. The truth is I have always known that deep down, but being young and foolish and wanting people to think well of me, and that my years of education were not wasted, I pretended otherwise.

I look back over the years and the theological discussions/arguments in which I participated. In many cases I rue the certainty which I exhibited, but didn't really possess, in order to appear smarter than I actually was. We like to argue things like theology as though we know for absolute certain. We don't. Life is a continuing series of mysteries that are really beyond us. We make approximations that help us make sense of things, and to an extent they are beneficial, but to assume that they are the whole truth and nothing but the truth is to stretch their value. I read the history of theological debates, discussing everything from the true nature of God to how many angels can dance on the head of a pin, and at this stage of my life I marvel at the energy used and the pain caused by wars and exclusions fomented by such distinctions. Then I review some of my "discussions" with my Baptist relatives and other such religious "opponents," and realize the similarities.

There are at least three stages to a healthy awareness of our own fallibility as far as I can see. (Notice the trinitarian formula.) First, I don't think I know everything. Second, I realize that I don't have to know everything. Then third, I shouldn't pretend to know everything.

There is something healthy about being able to respond to a question by saying "I don't know," or "I don't know for sure but it seems to me." Even better is this follow up, "How does it seem to you?" and then actually listening to their thoughts rather than ignoring the answer while formulating your next response.

We are handling things larger than ourselves and our understanding. Too often we have covered our uncertainty with an "attack-mode" to end the conversation. Sadly, often it also ends the possibility for growth and greater understanding.

So I have good news and bad news. The bad news: you don't know everything. The good news: you don't have to, at least not right now. "Farther along...."

Welcome To The NFL

It was after dark and I was driving back home on what, at that time of night, was a deserted road. I was returning from a board meeting at the second church on the two-point charge I had been serving for all of three months. Let's just say that the meeting had not gone well. One particular old-time member had spent the evening pretty much "eating me alive," to use a phrase I grew up with. He was not at all happy with almost anything that I had done. I found out later that it was even deeper than that, that he was not at all happy with who I was, having decided that I was a communist, based on the twin facts that I wore modest sideburns and did not begin the worship service every Sunday with bringing in the American flag and singing "America, the Beautiful."

So here I was driving slowly across what was known to the locals as "Toenail Trail" with my headlights the only interruption of the darkness. (You had to drive slowly because to do otherwise almost assured that you would gain one of the numerous deer in the area as a hood ornament.) There were no decent radio stations that I could pick up, and I had not yet bought that new invention, the eight track player that would later provide a distraction on similar journeys. So I was stuck with my anxieties. Here I was. This was the first time that I had full responsibility for a congregation, or in this case, two congregations. I had hardly started and already things were headed south. As I drove for what seemed forever, I considered what to do next, considering that this career was going up in smoke.

By the time I arrived home I had decided to call the District Superintendent to let him know all that had happened. And so the next morning, I did just that. As soon as he answered, I began pouring out my tale of woe. Charles Giesler was my DS then and a friend for years afterward. Often he was a sounding board and giver of advice. This was the first of many such occasions. I detailed what had happened, and how I did not think that it was fair, and that I did not know what I was supposed to do. He listened, and when I paused he asked "Are you through?" I answered, "Yes, I guess." "Well," he said, "Welcome to the NFL," and with that he hung up the phone. In other words, this is the big leagues. It will not always be easy. In fact, ease may be only an occasional reality, and fairness is often only in the eye of the beholder.

Another great lesson: just because you are doing what you think you are called to do, just because you think you are doing what you ought to do, does not mean that people will always necessarily be happy. Sometimes it is something you do that upsets them. Sometimes it is something in their own lives that they project on to you. Your calling is to do the best you can as faithfully as you can. If it works out, great. If not, well, welcome to the NFL.

But Who Gets The Credit

This is another bit of wisdom from the late Dr. Ted Richardson, one of several older pastors who mentored me in my early years right out of seminary. I remember him saying in his unique way, "It is amazing what you can accomplish when you don't care who gets the credit."

Those were good words to hear when just starting out, when I was trying to be noticed, when I was trying to "make a name for myself" (while remaining humble, of course). And when Ted's words were my operating principle, I must admit that things went well, or at least better. They went better, I think, because they are more in line with reality and our calling.

You see, none of us make it on our own. As I look back over the years and the various congregations I have served, there were always people who were invaluable to what we were able to do. Simply because I was the pastor I got much of the credit, but I would have been lost had they not been there standing at my shoulder and covering my backside. In fact, at times, I was a bit embarrassed when people would talk about "my" accomplishments when I knew it was not just me, but the people around me who were making possible all that was taking place.

At some point, I began to intentionally point to others, to acknowledge their importance to all that was taking place (not because I was overly humble, but because I realized that it was the truth) and in most cases an interesting thing happened. Things went even better, which taught me something else that of course I should have known and should have been better at doing. People who know themselves to be appreciated usually strive to do even more, and in that striving they benefit the whole operation.

Which leads me to this: we are not finally judged by how well we as individuals do, but by what we accomplish together. And that is true of any group, be it congregation or volunteer group or team or family, you name it. If we are continually pointing to ourselves, the strength of the group is diminished. If, on the other hand, we acknowledge the many contributions of others, the group is strengthened and accomplishes more.

It boils down to this: "It is amazing what you can accomplish when you don't care who gets the credit." Thanks again, Ted.

The Value Of Story

Once a group of engineers built a super computer. They were continually amazed at all the things that it could do. After days of having their expectations exceeded, they decided to pose this question to their creation: "Will a computer ever think like a human being?" The machine whirred and its lights flashed, and then came the answer: "That reminds me of a story."

Central to our humanity and the way we understand things is the use of story.

Dr. Darrell Gray was my first boss after I graduated from seminary. He hired me virtually sight unseen, most likely on the recommendation of my pastor from high school, Sam Fore. For over two years I worked for him and he mentored me, giving me the benefit of a lifetime of experience in ministry.

I had taken a course at Duke, taught by Dr. Charles Rice, which focused on the value of preaching from literature, but Darrell was the first preacher from whom I really learned the value of story or image. His sermons often began with, or centered around, a story that engaged the listener and opened them to the truth Darrell was hoping to share, or even maybe another truth of the listeners' own devising. Story can do that.

About the same time I became acquainted with the work of Dr. Fred Craddock who was a master of using story to preach. I was privileged to hear him preach at Annual Conference and later to attend a workshop on preaching one wonderful day at Laurel Heights UMC in San Antonio. I also read his books. It was Craddock who introduced the idea that in hearing a story, one has the chance to "overhear" the Gospel. As we are involved in the story, a greater truth becomes apparent. In fact, I recall that Jesus used the same device.

So over the years I have been on the lookout for great stories to use in preaching, but in that same time frame I have become aware of the importance of stories as a way of communicating what we are about in other settings. Sharing stories about how individuals within a congregation are ministering in their own settings opens to people who hear those stories the possibility that they too might be in ministry in their own daily lives. Stories about how actions of a group impacting one single life or family lets people know that something is happening in the world because they gather. Stories remind us of where we have been and, more importantly, where we might go.

We all are collectors of stories. We just need to be more intentional about it, whether or not we ever write a sermon. Stories can tell us who we are, and give us a vision of who we might become.

It's Okay Not To Believe All The Time

We don't like to say this out loud, but there are times when our faith is not all that strong. We keep it to ourselves because, I mean, what would people think? But the truth is that most of us, if not all of us, go through stretches where our faith is strained by the stuff life throws our way. And most of us, in the midst of the awareness of this weakening of faith, feel guilty about it. We worry about ourselves, and we worry about how God will deal with such foolishness.

Allow me to offer this word of comfort. Welcome to the human scene. You are not God, and you are not Jesus. (In fact some portions of the gospels seem to indicate that Jesus had some rough patches as well.) We cannot be one hundred percent on the believing scale all the time. There is too much we don't know. There is too much we don't understand. There are too many times when life is just too hard.

Sometimes you have to run on the momentum that has already been built up. Sometimes you have to act out of the basic idea that this is "just the right thing to do." Sometimes you have to plow through the dark valley until you can climb up the hillside to get a new and brighter vision.

Frederick Buechner in his book <u>Speak What We Feel (Not What We Ought To Say)</u> recounts some of the circumstances of the lives of Gerald Manley Hopkins, Mark Twain, G.K. Chesterton, and William Shakespeare. In so doing he gives us the often tragic backstory to these authors' greatest works. At the same time, he also shares some of his own pain concerning the loss of his father by suicide.

He ends the book with these words which should serve as an admonition to us all: "Take heart…even at the unlikeliest moments. Fear not. Be alive. Be merciful. Be human. And most unlikely of all: Even when you can't believe, even if you don't believe at all, even if you shy away at the sound of his name, be Christ."

May it be so for us all.

God Is More Than You Know

When you read this title, I imagine your response is akin to that of my grandchildren: "Well, duh, Gramps." And most of us would affirm that, but then we immediately go about constructing our personal images of God, usually images that we can handle, images that allow us to stay pretty much where we are.

We need to remember (a la Marcus Borg and many others) that all of our descriptions of God are in the form of simile. Since God is beyond us, we describe God by saying "God is like a Father or a King or a shepherd." Each of these, and so many others, help us describe an aspect of this central reality that is beyond our ability to totally describe. The problem comes when we concretize our similes, that is to say we forget the "like" part. God is no longer "like" a king or father or shepherd. God "is" what we have used to describe God's reality. Worse, we then exclude those that others have used, believing that only ours have value. That decision on our part is limiting to our greater understanding of the nature of God. For example, if the only image of God you will allow is father, then if your experience of father is someone who was always at work and emotionally separate from the family, then that shapes your vision of God.

To me it comes down to this. God is greater than anything that we can understand; so, by definition, all of our images will be inadequate, limited by our human experience and perspective. As a result, sooner or later, most of our images of God will fall short. We will become discouraged with them, or we will bend them around to fit our experience and/or prejudices.

Years ago in a segment of the TV series "Mash", the supply lines were cut to the Unit and they were forced to have the same meals day after day. Finally the place erupted. Led, of course, by Hawkeye (Alan Alda's character) they paraded around the mess tent chanting "We want something else! We want something else!"

After a while we get that way with our self-created images of God. We sense their inadequacies and "we want something else." In short, when we create God in our own image, a God that looks like us, acts like us, and thinks like us, we have a god that is inadequate to the task of changing us, or even more importantly, of saving us. By that I mean literally giving our best life to us, giving us something out of which to live.

I need to remember; you need to remember; we need to remember together that God is more than we know, that we only occasionally touch the hem of his garment. We need to be grateful for that touch, but we cannot assume that is all that there is to the experience, or that ours is the only real experience. There is always more to God than we know.

Don't Let Me Resign In October

A wise pastor friend of mine once told a group of us that he had instructed his wife never to let him resign in the month of October.

That might seem strange to those outside of the operating structure of the organizational church, but October is a hard time. That is the month when in the United Methodist Church, and I believe in other denominations as well, a number of issues arise. The annual Church Conference looms ahead and with it the countless forms that need to be filled out after first being deciphered. (We seem to work at making these things more and more complicated.) Before the forms can be filled out, the officers for the coming year have to be recruited and nominated, and the budget must be set. Before the budget can be established, there needs to be the annual pledge campaign. Few lay people are aware of the depth of anxiety this annual exercise brings with it. Not only are programs affected, but the lives of staff people are greatly impacted and the pastor knows those people and lives with them day-to-day.

So there is all this organizational stuff, and once all this is taken care of, or more accurately, during the same time this is all being taken care of, planning is going on for the high holy season of Advent-Christmas with all that entails.

I do not write this in hopes that people will feel sorry for their pastor, although any compassion would certainly be appreciated. These words are written mainly to pastors, staff, and those in positions of leadership. October should not come as a surprise. It comes around every year. I knew that when I was pastoring, and yet it always seemed to sneak up on me.

Now a logical response would be to prepare as much as one can ahead of time. Lists could be compiled. Form letters could be written. Plans for the form and shape of the finance campaign could be chosen. Preliminary lists of names could be drawn up in light of the offices that will need to be filled. The Advent texts could be considered again and basic worship plans made. As I said, that is the logical response. The problem is that the life of the church is ongoing. There is always some immediate claim that seems to preclude preparing for those future claims. I know that, but I still would advise carving out some time for the future requirements in the midst of the daily claims on our time. I would also suggest "farming out" those responsibilities. Let someone else handle the format of the financial campaign and report back their chosen options. Let someone else compile a list of active and involved people who might be the current and future leaders of the congregation. In other words, delegate.

But more importantly, take care of your soul. There is a need for reflection time, for times of prayer. You need to keep track of who you are and what is your real calling. You are more than a denominational pencil pusher. You are a child of God who has been called to be in this place at this time. Live out of that calling.

And finally, remember that November also comes every year. You have made it through all this before. Odds are very good that you will make it through again, and there will be the joy of Advent and Christmas. But for the moment, if you are married, or if you are single and have a trusted friend, remind them to watch out for you during this busy time, and make sure they don't let you resign during the month of October.

Happy And Unhappy

Years ago Kennon Callahan, writing in <u>Twelve Keys for an Effective Church</u>, made what for me has been a very helpful distinction about happy and unhappy people.

We often make a mistake. We assume that if we fix the things that people say make them unhappy, they will be happy. Callahan points out that this is not necessarily the case. Often, once those things are fixed, those people are just no longer unhappy.

His contention is that happiness comes from meaning and purpose, from knowing one's own life is being made better and others' lives as well. Often the concerns we hear about in church are not about life-changing things. "There is not enough parking. The air conditioner is not working. I don't know the hymns. There are not enough restrooms." Upon hearing these and others, we sense the unhappiness, and we believe what needs to be done is to make the appropriate fixes and all will be well. People will be happy.

But what if it is not the air conditioning that is keeping people from an experience of the presence of God. What if they had their own reserved parking space by the front door, but still went home empty. This is where Callahan's distinctions are helpful. True, they are no longer unhappy about whatever, but there is little to be excited about because their lives are not being changed. They are no longer inconvenienced, but they are still facing a feeling of empty.

Callahan goes on to say that there are many things which enrich peoples' lives. He lists worship, study, mission involvement, as well as others. Herein lies the possibility for a person's life to be changed and for that person to change the lives of others. Here one's faith is made real. Here is where one is happy in the fullest sense of the word.

People will come to you with things that make them unhappy, and those things need to be fixed. But don't assume that will make them happy. You just might be relieving a gripe. There is more to the job. We need to offer opportunities for their very lives to be make different. They need a greater sense of who they are and who they are called to be. In that realization, there lies the possibility of true happiness.

From Darkness To Light

Nancy called sometime in the afternoon telling us that her husband Bill was sick with what looked and felt like the flu. That was of course troubling, but what made it worse was the fact that Bill's sister was arriving at the Houston Airport at 11:00 p.m. that very night, and they had planned to drive from San Antonio to pick her up. Nancy said they were still going to make the trip with Bill bedded down in the back of their station wagon. That did not sound like a great idea to me considering how Bill was feeling, and so I volunteered to drive her to Houston allowing him to stay at home and rest.

We left in the dark and drove the four hours the trip required, arrived in Houston in plenty of time, met Bill's sister, and began the trip home. I know it seems silly to say, but it seemed darker on the return trip. Interstate 10 to Houston has never been one of my favorite stretches of road, but at least in the day time there is scenery to break up the monotony. On that dark night there were no such breaks. The only thing visible was the highway in front of us. Exhaustion was setting in. Conversation lagged. I found my mind playing tricks on me. I would think that I had surely gone twenty miles only to see a sign indicating I had only traveled two or three. It seemed the trip would never end.

I recall a similar trip. I was driving back from Duke Divinity School. I had left about 10:30 in the morning right after my oral final in Hebrew. The memory of that one-on-one experience with Dr. Steinspring and my faltering Hebrew, coupled with the anticipation that I was driving home to get married, had me wide awake—at least for the first six or seven hours. My plan was to stop in Atlanta to spend the night, but I arrived there at three in the afternoon and decided that it was too early to stop. The problem was that after Atlanta there were not a lot of places that I wanted to stop, driving across the South in the late 1960's. So for the next eighteen hours I continued on. The same experience of darkness that I would experience later on the trip to Houston occurred on that night, probably the longest, loneliest night of my life. In retrospect, it was incredibly silly to make such a run. I struggled desperately from two a.m. until six to keep awake. Finally the sun began to come up, and with it came new alertness. I could see things. I could sense progress. Finally I pulled up to Fara's front door, and made it to the couch downstairs where I could sleep.

Both of these times have places in my memory. I remember them because of what happened at the end of the journeys. In one, Bill's sister was delivered safely, and in the other I got home and one week later was married. But from both of these there is also this abiding memory of the darkness, of having no change of scene to break the monotony, of the exhaustion that comes from just plodding on. I don't think the lights of San Antonio ever looked so good than they did at about 3 a.m. I don't know that I was ever more grateful for the glimmers of light that promised a new day as I neared the outskirts of Houston.

Sometimes our lives are like that. We plod along just racking up what seems like never-ending miles without any real sense of progress and wondering if we will ever arrive where we are headed. Then finally there is a light on the horizon. Things become at least somewhat clearer. We can see more of what is going by us, and if we are really lucky, we finally get the sense that we are really and truly heading home.

It's Odd What We Remember;
It's Odd What We Forget

Who knows why we remember what we remember? Why is it that certain things stay with us while others slip away?

It was the annual gathering of men at Big Bend. Everyone had come together at the campsite in the Chisos Mountain Basin. Vehicles were unloaded, tents were set up, gear was stored. Several people walked by my just established temporary residence and asked what I was going to do now. One group was heading off on a hike in one direction and another was planning a different trek. I remember answering "Nothing." They seemed surprised by that answer. I remember being a bit surprised at their surprise.

All of us had traveled some eight hours to get away for a few days from busy schedules that required more of us than we had to offer. We had come to this beautiful, almost mystical, natural wonder, and immediately there was the urge to set about doing something. It was just like home in a different setting.

Everyone scattered to the four winds leaving me alone in the campsite with a book I had brought and some precious unscheduled time on my hands. I sat in the middle of the campsite in the middle of the basin surrounded on all sides with incredible mountains. I read for a few moments, but mainly I thought. Did I come up with the answers to the world's problems? No, but I did have some time to myself with myself, and I remember that. I remember deciding that. It's odd what we remember.

Lately I have altered my schedule somewhat. I am a morning person. My wife is not. She reads at night. I have started reading in the morning.

Before I look at the news with its overflow of depressing information, I pick up Frederick Buechner or Marcus Borg or John Dominic Crossen or Richard Rohr, or others. I have been interested at how some of these authors' autobiographical revelations parallel my own, and I find comfort in that as I reflect on my own meandering faith development.

I say all of that to say this: I wish I had remembered to carve out such early morning moments as these more often in my life. I know why I didn't. I was always too busy. There were all these things to do. I did not have time to take stock of my situation because I was buried in my situation. What would have been different with some regular infusion of perspective?

I know that now. Really, I suppose, I knew it all along. It's odd what we remember. It's odd--no, it's sad--what we forget.

Some Christmases Are
Just Harder Than Others

We have such high expectations for the season of Christmas. Even those who are not particularly religious look forward to the reuniting with friends and family, and sometimes the season lives up to and even exceeds our expectations…but not always. Some years circumstances combine to make the experience so much less than we had hoped.

Maybe it has always been so. Think back to the Christmas narrative itself. Surely Mary had higher expectations for the birth of her first-born than the accommodations where the delivery took place. I mean, given the build up with the angel Gabriel's announcement, surely she expected more than a stable. But a stable it was.

Christmas always takes place in the midst of a particular environment, and this year's environment has not been particularly conducive. For one thing, where we live it has been incredibly warm, which does not fit with all the cards with pictures of snowy landscapes we have received.

It is a hard time in the world right now, but it is the world of which we are a part. There has always been hate loose among us, but because of the internet and other forms of mass communication, we are more aware of its presence and more frightened by its possibilities. Those of us who have lived long enough begin to see patterns from the past being played out again, and remembering how they turned out the first time puts us on edge.

On a more personal level we have lost some people close to us, and people dear to us have lost people close to them. We feel their pain and our own in the midst of this season of hoped-for joy. Further, things are not what we might wish in our various relationships. Hurt colors our celebrations of the season. We are more aware of distance. People we love are too far away to see, people we love are too separate for our liking.

In Luke's Gospel, Mary did not get to choose the circumstances for the birth of the child. We do not get to choose the circumstances of this Christmas, but we can do what she did. We can make the best of what is.

The Christ came into the world, a world not ready for him, then or now. But it is its very unreadiness that necessitates his coming. It is our personal unreadiness that necessitates his coming. And come he does in the most unexpected of places, the stables and mangers of our existence.

May we all recognize him when we see him.

Lives That Matter

I received word recently that E.O. Williams died. Don't feel bad that you missed it; it appeared in none of the local papers; there was no mention on the local news. No, for most people it did not cause the slightest ripple, but it did to me because I knew E.O. Williams.

E.O. (that's what everybody called him) was the weekend sexton (which is a nice word for janitor) at Laurel Heights United Methodist Church for as long as anyone could remember. He had retired from that position several years ago, but his memory remained alive in the hearts of those who frequented the halls and worship spaces of that congregation.

To me, he was an almost Ghandi-like figure. He was a small, wiry man with a wonderfully warm smile and a great laugh (really it was almost a cackle as he leaned on the counter right outside the kitchen). I would always arrive early at the Church on Sunday mornings or on Saturdays before a wedding and he would be there and things would be ready. On Sunday morning that meant that the coffee was brewing, and most of us know how important that is. On more than a few occasions we would have conversations about this and that, nothing that mattered a great deal. It was just fun to be around him.

Apparently I was not the only one who felt that way. On the occasion of his 100th birthday, there was a grand party for him in the fellowship hall that he had so lovingly cared for and prepared so that all would be ready for those who gathered on Sunday morning. That day someone else prepared it for him.

He died at the age of 102, and I wonder at all that he saw in that lifetime. You see E.O. was a black man who worked in what was for years a lily-white church. And besides all the scientific changes and technological advances, he lived through a hard time for black people in this country in general and Texas in particular. Now I wish that I had talked to him about all that. Maybe I just took his graceful presence as a given, without even pausing to think how remarkable it was, considering all that he must have gone through.

There is something about a life that is well-lived. It touches people, even people who are very different from you. It offers another possibility, another vision other than the angry, fearful spirits that so often dominate our common lives together. Being in such a presence gives us hope that there is another possibility for our living. Such lives are a treasure.

E.O. Williams died, but his long life taught those around him. I know most of you reading this did not know him, but I did, and the people of Laurel Heights United Methodist Church did, and we are all richer for that experience.

I Would Know Him Anywhere

Sometimes your mouth makes promises your mind can't keep. I have learned that "I would know him anywhere" is one of those promises.

I have known her since forever. We grew up in the same town. We attended the same Church. For a time she dated one of my best friends in high school. We ended up going to the same college. She was also a beautiful person outside and in, and thus hard to miss. I am convinced that I would have said to myself or whoever might be listening "I would know her anywhere."

Some time ago (time tends to run together lately) I was attending a meeting at which I was supposed to make a presentation. Before the meeting this very attractive lady walked up to me and began one of those conversations that indicate that she not only knows you but knows you very well. I have become used to such exchanges over the years. One of the things about preaching is that people think they know you because you have been talking to them week in and week out. I was trying to place which church or what setting it might have been where we had met. Then she introduced herself to someone else and immediately I knew who she was. Needless to say I felt embarrassed, but I tried to pick up where we left off so many years ago with conversation about where she was living, how her brothers were, and other such conversational gambits.

Now I think I know why this happened. She was in a setting where I did not expect her to be. I have had this happen before with others, but none quite so striking or embarrassing. It was a Conference meeting. It should have crossed my mind that someone with her capabilities would end up in such a setting of leadership but of course it did not. She was gracious, never letting on that she realized what had happened.

I move from that occasion to a theological reflection brought on by Matthew 25, especially that portion where people ask Jesus "When did we see you?" It appears to me that they are acting out of the same state of mind. "Oh, I would know you anywhere." But the truth is that too often we would know him only if he showed up where we expected him to appear. It might be in the midst of a tremendous performance of some great musical work or a special sermon. It might be in a quiet church setting where you are all alone with your thoughts and your God. He might present himself as you read a beautifully written insightful answer to one of the countless questions that haunt our collective religious life. We would see him if he showed up at the appropriate time and place.

But what if he doesn't? What if the setting is different than we expected? The text referenced earlier mentions the poor, the imprisoned, the sick, among others as places for possible sightings. Would we recognize him there? Or would his disguise be too effective for us to see through? I fear too often that has been the case for me.

And so my bragging response would need to be changed. I can no longer say "I would know him anywhere." Rather I have to say "How could I have missed him?"

Specific, But Not Necessarily Correct

I was not particularly looking forward to the hospital visit. I did not know the person I was going to see. He was not a part of my congregation, but his son was and the son had asked me to go see his Dad who was very ill. And so I was walking down the halls of the hospital to his room.

They must have warned him that I was coming because he was armed and ready. You see he was an active member of a congregation which operated out of a much more conservative brand of theology than that with which I was comfortable. And it was soon clear that he wanted to straighten me out on some things.

I had barely gotten into the door, introduced myself, and asked how he was when he started in. He began by asking me when I thought Jesus was coming back. I responded that I did not know, which was, of course, exactly what he wanted to hear. "Well, let me tell you…" and with that he launched into his dissertation which was comprised of a vast selection of portions of scriptures mainly from the Old Testament seasoned with some references from the Book of Revelation. It did not take me long to note that he had chosen select words from the chosen passages often ignoring the context from which those words came. His presentation went on for several minutes (It actually seemed much longer than that.) He paused, and with a satisfied look, he asked "What do you think about that?"

I thought a moment hardly knowing where to begin. It was wonderfully specific, representing a lot of effort. I just didn't think that it was correct. My response was something like this. "Well, I don't agree with all you said, but it takes more than one horse in order to have a race." Then I asked him, "What do you do with that passage that says we will not know the day or the hour of his coming." Without a pause he looked at me and said, "Oh, we don't know the day or the hour, but we are pretty sure about the month and the year."

Over the last several weeks I have been rereading several books preparing a class on the issue of the presence of evil in a good world or why does God allow pain. One of my sources was C.S. Lewis. I admit that his book The Problem of Pain still represents a struggle for me to plow through. The tight reasoning and the attention to detail reminds me of some of the theology books I was required to read in seminary. That coupled with my earlier experience in that hospital room brings me to this.

We struggle with the idea that God is beyond us. We believe that we want to understand God, but what I really think we want is to contain God within some manageable concepts. We want to know which buttons to push on the "God machine" in order for things to work out or to be comfortable that we are in line for a "room by the pool in the heavenly Hilton." And so we come up with our ideas of God and we dig though the scriptures seeking support for the idea of God that we already like.

The problem is this. God is beyond us. I believe it was Anselm who wrote centuries ago that "God is that than which nothing greater can be conceived." We just hang our lives on the great summary statements. "Love the Lord your God with all your heart, soul, mind, and strength and your neighbor as yourself." "What does the Lord require of you, but to do justice, to love mercy, and to walk humbly with your God." As I get older, I have the sense that if we focus on that, a lot of the other stuff will take care of itself.

Now, am I suggesting that we sure never try to understand God and how all of this works? I am not. I am just reminding myself and you that now matter how specific your references, how minute your research, there is still more to God than we know. God is finally mystery, and we live before that mystery. The truth is that we don't know the day or the hour. In fact, we don't even know the month and the year.

Love, Lost

As I look across the spectrum of our collective lives, I fear that we are continually losing track of something, something important, something that holds us together.

When I was in the seventh grade, Mrs. Tucker, our language arts teacher, would require us to memorize a passage from some form of literature each six weeks. One such period the assignment was the thirteenth chapter of First Corinthians. (You can immediately tell how long ago that was.) I have, of course, come across this text many times since and even preached on it on many occasions, but the closing words still get my attention. The first time they did so because it meant that I was through reciting it to Mrs. Tucker and did not have to worry about that assignment any more. But even today, with no such requirement staring me in the face, they matter.

"And now abide these three: faith, hope, and love, but the greatest of these is love." (I Corinthians 13:13)

It seems to me that there is an essential truth with which we are losing contact. Somehow in our worlds where we are divided by politics, class, race, and, yes, even religion, we are losing track of that which holds us together. We are much more concerned about points of difference than we are about that which unites us.

Lately, I have been reading President Jimmy Carter's book, <u>Living Faith</u>, which was published in 1992. It was given to me in 1996 by Lamar Youngblood (at least I hope he intended to give it to me since I still have it after all these years.) For many folks Lamar was the face of First United Methodist Church, Austin. He greeted people at the front door and made it his business to try to make sure they felt welcome and worked to integrate them into the life of the congregation. He did the same for me when I moved to Austin in 1994. Seeing his name in the front of the book when I pulled it down from the shelf brought back so many memories

But back to Carter's book and these words that I found in his introduction:

> "Somewhat to my surprise, this has become a book whose core is love-the love that is possible among those who are closely related, among strangers allied by a common dream or faith, and even between people who begin by despising each other but find a way to see the image of God in each other's humanity."

That's what we are losing. We are more likely to keep account of wrongs, intended or otherwise. We are more focused on winning, or just not losing, rather than the general betterment of all. Too many issues are approached from the point of view of "how can I get advantage for me and mine out of this?" The result is that the fabric of life is continually being torn apart. As we all sit in our individual houses, watching our chosen news channels, reading from our personalized reading lists, and building up our individual resentments, increasingly there is no us, there is me and mine, and maybe finally there is just me.

Paul got it right. In the midst of a world of possibilities, there are three things that abide, that stay, that finally hold us together. They are faith, hope, and love, but the greatest of these is love. We lose track of that reality to our peril.

From The Bleachers

A lesson from my senior year in high school: it is a great thing to be a part of a winning team; it is much harder to be part of a team that continually loses. I learned that because I was a part of both that year.

In football we never won. The season was a struggle from start to finish. I still remember the one sentence pre-season summary of our team's prospects in the Valley Morning Star, the area paper of record. We showed up in the last sentence of the last paragraph of a long article describing our district with this brief but accurate description; "2 and 8 last year, must rebuild."

It was like the difference between night and day when basketball season started. We went from being the district doormat to being a team from which much was expected and which lived up to most of those expectations. (We did not make it to the state tournament, a disappointment which still haunts many of us.)

It is interesting to have been a part of both of those experiences-one of victory and one of defeat. Some of the same people were a part of both teams. And one of the things that stays with me is the response from the bleachers.

During football season you dreaded the trip to town on Saturday morning after Friday night's game because you knew that you were going to have to listen to everyone's critique as to what you were doing wrong, how you weren't even trying, or how you just were not in shape (this usually said by someone who was some 100 pounds overweight). It was almost as though they thought you started out each week determined to figure out a way to humiliate yourself and them.

But as soon as the gun sounded on the last Friday night game, the whole atmosphere changed. Football was over, now it was basketball season. People wanted to talk to you about how well things were going and what a great job you were doing.

The problem, you see, is that I was the same person. The uniform was different. The equipment was different. But I was still me. I worked just as hard at football as I did at basketball. The results were just different. Who knows why? Maybe we were just better suited to the speedier game. Maybe we had more consistent coaching. Who can say?

I think about that now afresh. My grandson is in the high school band, and it is an incredible high school band program. Winning awards is an expected part of each year. (The same was true of my high school band. It was said that most people came to our games for the halftime show.)

We started attending the home games to see them march. Coincidently, the football program is also one of the best in the state, and we have seen more than a few games that were really over by half-time, so that we could go home after the band had performed without much worry that we would miss anything.

As I sat in the stands watching, I must admit to mixed emotions. I am delighted that the team is doing so well, but I have been on the other side. I think about the kids who have also worked hard so many weeks before to prepare for this game. I think about their hopes that this might be the night when they exceed all expectations. I identify with the gradual slump in their shoulders and their spirit as they realize that, yet again, they will be defeated, that this will not be that night.

We have become a society of people sitting in the bleachers, or watching television, or sitting in the pews. We quickly judge who are the winners and losers based on our particular expectations. We are quick to find fault with those who fail us, and equally quick to excuse those who make us feel good about ourselves.

Sometimes it's hard to remember that often both those who win and those who lose are trying hard and giving their best. Winners are not always paragons of effort and the ones they beat are not always slackers. Most often both are just doing the best they can. Trust me on that. I have been in both camps.

Maybe we can remember that as we watch from the bleachers or the couch or the pews, as we offer our harsh critiques of those who are struggling to make sense of it all, to create some order out of the chaos, to make the world better. We need to remember that some will be successful and some won't. Some will meet our personal expectations; others will fall short. As we watch, we need to give credit for effort and intention. We need to restrain our tendency to divide into categories of winners and losers. And finally we need to do what we can do to help, to support, and to encourage all those who struggle on our behalf.

Whose Side Are You On?

Whose side are you on? Increasingly that seems to be the question these days. It may have always been this way, but with the supposed blessings of the internet and 24-hour "news" channels we are just more aware of our differences.

As I look at the quagmire that we have become, several principles seem to become obvious.

The first is what I would call a "spectrum," or the "us and them" theory. It seems to me that we all reside on a spectrum from left to right. The thing that has become clear is that any one who resides inside of "us" on the spectrum is one of "them." If you are not as liberal as I am, then you must be a conservative or "one of them." The same is true for conservatives. As you move nearer and nearer the center, the "thems" fall on both sides of you. I am not as conservative as you, so you are one of "them." At the same time I am not as liberal as someone else so they are "thems" too. They are just a different group of "thems."

To make things worse, we are bitterly defensive of our position on the spectrum. It can be argued as to whether the source of that is our certainty or our uncertainty, but it is there whatever the cause.

A second principle is the "circle" principle, and it is certainly not new with me. It holds that the afore-mentioned spectrum is not linear; it is circular. The extremes really end up meeting each other. The odd thing is we may not sense this because we are standing back to back, looking in opposite directions, but in spite of our differences we view the world through similar eyes.

On the Sunday evening after 9/11, we had previously scheduled a professor from Rice to come to our congregation to talk about fundamentalism. In spite of that horrible week with all its uncertainty, we continued with the plan to have him speak. Something he said that night has stayed with me. He told us that all fundamentalists (Jews, Christians, and Muslims) view the world the same way. They have made the same divisions of good and evil. They just disagree as to the source of those realities.

So whose side are you on? What are the differences that you have chosen that allow you to separate yourself from those with whom you differ? What are the ones that I have chosen?

Might I suggest another, more helpful, question? What are the things that we hold in common? What are the beliefs whose importance we share? On what do we have to build relationships? Are they not more important than those we have chosen to tear us apart?

It is probably a bad time to raise these questions, it being our quadrennial political season when people are basing their various candidacies on how they are different, but maybe not. We are approaching our quadrennial General Conference in the United Methodist Church, and the same issues hold true. Maybe we could do a better job as citizens, and as people of faith, were we to begin with what we hold dear together. Sensing that common understanding and its importance, with the awareness that we are finally on the same side, maybe we could then more faithfully deal with our differences.

What Were You Thinking, God?

I believe it was Woody Allen who once said, ""If it turns out that there is a God...the worst that you can say about him is that basically he's an underachiever."

This came to mind the other day while I was reading Jimmy Carter's book, Living Faith. Suddenly a bit of history jumped off the page, something, that if I had known it, had slipped into my unconscious. In 1966 Carter ran for governor of Georgia and lost. What made it hard for him to take then, and for me to take now, is that he was beaten by Lester Maddox, an avowed racist who campaigned waving an ax handle that he had used to beat any blacks who might patronize his place of business.

Some thing about that result offends me. That was not how it was supposed to work out. Good is supposed to triumph over evil. But to my way of thinking, it certainly did not in that circumstance. The good and decent man is supposed to win out over the inherent evil of racism, but it did not happen.

Of course, that is not the only occasion where such was the case. There have been many more, and many less, serious breaches of what I consider to be the proper moral order, but their being so numerous does not detract from the difficulty they present.

"What were you thinking, God? Why was this allowed? With all the details you have to deal with, did this just slip by unnoticed?

Of course, at the base of all of this is our image of God. The trouble is the job description that we have designated to the Most High. The problem is that we construct a view of God and then try to bend both life and God into a shape that fits that view.

For years now, I have been reading and re-reading Leslie Weatherhead's book The Will of God. Another helpful source has been Harold Kushner's When Bad Thing Happen to Good People. From both of these authors, an important idea comes forth. Summarized, it is this. "God allows what God does not intend." Because we are given free choice, we can choose to do what God intends, or we can choose otherwise. Often we have done the latter, and we have to live with the result. That is tragic enough, but more tragic is the fact that others have to live with the results of the choices that we make.

We can look back over history and pick particularly disastrous decisions that have affected a much wider circle of people than just the original deciders. The Holocaust comes to mind, as does 9/11. But there are countless others. People decide on a selfish or careless, basis, quite contrary to the intention of God, and others suffer for their choices.

In truth, we make similar choices. Oh, the results may not make the paper. Maybe just a few people are affected, but they are still choices contrary to the intention of God. And so we are where we are, and we take others with us.

So do we believe that God has washed God's hands of the whole affair? Are we stuck here on our own? Is God in Woody Allen's words, "an underachiever?" Again Weatherhead is helpful to me. He posits that God still works within the circumstances that we create through our choices, whether those choices were a part of the original intention or not. God still works toward God's ultimate intention of bringing all creation to the one who creates in the first place.

It seems likely to me that Allen has it wrong. It is not God who is the underachiever at all. Rather it is we who make choices, small and large, that cause unfairness and pain. God does not hinder our choosing; God continually works with us to heal the results of our choices.